The Third Burden:
My True Story of Defeating Discrimination in the Workplace

By

Eric Hughes

WENDIBRAND PUBLISHING CO., INC
WASHINGTON, DC 20020

Some of the names used in this book have been changed to protect the identities of people involved in my job discrimination cases.

ISB #0-9719131-0-2
Printed in the United States of America

First Printing

For Information or to order additional books, please write:
WendiBrand Publishing Co., Inc.
P.O. Box 6710
Washington, D.C. 20020
1-866-850-6396
Or visit our web site — www.discrimrelief.com

This book is dedicated to my beloved deceased parents, Christopher D. Hughes and Helen W. Richardson, both of whom provided a character-building life for me while growing up in Perth Amboy, New Jersey.

Dedication

The late Ernest Hazell, Cedric Hodge, Benjamin (Butch) Meyers, Lawrence (Larry) Bryant, Arthur Graham and Joseph Davis were six of my closest friends while growing up in Perth Amboy, NJ. I dedicate this book in their memory.

I also dedicate this book to my children, Tracy and Wendy; and my grandchildren, Chase, Riley, Brandon and Logan, and pray that their lives will be free from discrimination in all forms in the new millennium.

Finally, I dedicate this book to all black Americans, and to people of color throughout the world. We must confront discrimination whenever it occurs or face the prospects of continuous oppression.

Contents

Foreword

This book is about the horrendous treatment I endured as a black man in the workplace of the U.S. federal government. It is far from being an uncommon story and such injustices continue today. Few minorities who consider charging our federal government with racial discrimination initiate and pursue the requisite career-threatening and exhausting process to its end. I spent more than 15 years fighting racial discrimination in two Cabinet-level agencies of our federal government...and won! My victories were unique in that they were not complaints of class discrimination, a process which enables numerous employees to collectively sue their agency by alleging to have been adversely affected by personnel policy or practice which discriminates against the group based on their common race, color, religion, sex, national origin, age, or disability. They were struggles I undertook myself, a much more difficult process because it's one person against the U.S. government, a daunting task. Affording an attorney, the uncertainty of the outcome, and retaliation and stress are but a few reasons why there are not more cases in the system. Faced with all of these challenges and obstacles, I never wavered in my pursuit of justice.

My story is important because I show, by example, that victories against racial discrimination are possible. In addition, it needs to be known because it stands to inspire and empower countless persons to also take action and seek justice. My experiences demonstrate the meaning of "staying the course" and "perseverance."

I've been asked many times, "How did you do it?" For certain, the strength of character my parents instilled in me enabled me to persistently and successfully battle the racial discrimination I was subjected to. They taught me never to countenance unfair treatment as long as there is some way to oppose it. I read about how black veterans who served in World War I, World War II, Korea and Vietnam faced discrimination in gaining employment and finding decent housing for their families, and it was hurtful reading. Many of these veterans were disabled serving this country, yet even they were relegated to second class citizenship. As a veteran who also served this country for 4 years, I vowed I would never accept discrimination in any form.

I read and was inspired by John Hope Franklin's book, "From Slavery to Freedom," which gave me an eye-opening history lesson about black Americans. I was equally inspired by the actions of the four students from the Negro Agricultural and Technical College in Greensboro, NC, who in 1960 began the sit-in movement for equal rights by sitting down at a public lunch counter even though they were refused service because they were black. I was motivated by Rosa Parks who in 1955 in Montgomery, Alabama, refused to give up her seat to a white man, which sparked one of the most successful boycotts in this country. The beatings and killings during the freedom marches of the 1960s deeply affected me. I marveled at the manner in which Dr. Martin Luther King, Jr., Malcom X and A. Phillip Randolph dedicated their careers to speaking out about the injustices against blacks. These people and their actions contributed to the passing of one of the most important laws for black Americans and other minorities in America: The Civil Rights Act of 1964, as amended.

I tell my story by looking at the ingredients of myself, given to me by my parents. They instilled in me the strength and character to fight for the principle of fairness in my life. Back in the 1930s and 1940s, they faced real adversity in their lives because during that period there were no laws that prohibited discrimination. They were continually denied decent housing, health care, equal employment opportunities and respect, but simply did the best they could and lived a life of quiet dignity. Their goal was to provide a better life for their children and teach us how to deal with society and resist unfairness in our lives.

I discuss my early years growing up in Perth Amboy, NJ, a blue collar city with a diversified population. It was truly a melting pot and, for the most part, we all lived in harmony. I spent my adolescent years in the company of whites both at school and at social functions and accepted racial diversity and integration as a way of life.

But as an adult, it was my military experience that shaped my thinking about race in America. For the first time in my life, I lived and worked with white people who hated me because of my race. Although I survived those troubling experiences by focusing on other activities, it was a rude awakening for me after growing up in the north in a diverse and integrated environment.

After my military years, I entered civilian life as a federal employee full of hope and potential. Armed with 4 years of military training in teletype and cryptography, I set out to be the best employee I could be. For the most part, I met my goals and objectives. However, during the early 1960s, I found a difficult road ahead of me with respect to career enhancement and opportunities. My 20-year career with the State Department yielded many achievements and, unfortunately, several disappointments.

The State Department case was truly a lesson in perseverance. In the five years prior to my filing a complaint, I persistently sought assistance from numerous high departmental officials in being reassigned to personnel or other administrative positions. What happened to me over those five years was far more serious than the typical "bureaucratic run-around" – it was the result of manipulative and evil behavior that these officials manifested. These were white officials in key administrative and management positions willing to promote and advance their white counterparts while simultaneously advising me, a highly qualified black employee, not to bother them with my pursuits. These were officials using public funds to advance their own careers and those of their friends, while denying minorities opportunity for advancement. They attempted to justify their actions by lying about how much they went out of their way to assist me, stating that I didn't want to compete and that all I wanted was a promotion. They even suggested that I find employment at another federal agency. They had no intention of ensuring that I received equal career advancement opportunities at the State Department. The cover-up did not stop there, as lies spread during the investigation of my case.

It is difficult to explain what I went through for the 12 years I fought for justice at the State Department. As difficult as it was, I am glad that I took a stand against racial discrimination because nothing good results from accepting injustice.

Having wrestled for the lengthy period it took to win the State Department case, I never had the faintest notion that two years after the settlement of that case, it would happen again. I found myself embroiled in a three-year struggle for justice at the U.S. Department of Commerce, National Oceanic and Atmospheric Administration, National Ocean Service. This case was a bitter and stressful experience. I survived by drawing on the strength of my upbringing, family and friends, the experience of the first case and

xi

vowing never to accept injustice as long as there was a way to oppose it.

While the issues were different than the State Department case, the actions of the officials who discriminated against me in this case were just as evil, even sick. I discuss the different positions I held, the schemes that management used to block me from selection to higher-paying positions, and the manner in which I countered their moves. Again, I prevailed after a bitter hearing before the U.S. Equal Employment Opportunity Commission and the same agency upheld my appeals decision.

Shortly after I retired, I walked into my garage where I had stored numerous files of case documents. I thought long and hard about the reasons I kept them and came to the realization that one day they would be useful. But I thought, "How can they be useful when they're just sitting on the shelves?" I decided that my long struggle was too important to remain within me with so many others going through similar turmoil. People need to know that they are not alone in the fight against racial discrimination in the workplace. For that reason, I decided to use the information I had filed away to write this book and try to help others understand what it takes to win racial discrimination cases. My message is: *We don't deserve the right to hate prejudice until we spend our lives opposing it.*

My hope is that this true story may become part of the legacy left to the children of all black Americans who grew up in the fifties, experienced the civil rights movement, and matured during the endless struggles to translate early legislative victories into the right to expect justice everyday of our lives. While the glorious battles of Dr. King and the civil rights movement brought about national laws forbidding unequal treatment of citizens based upon racial heritage, the majesty of his dream will never be realized by regulations alone. The legislative victories he saw in his lifetime, no matter how righteous and glorious, were not enough to fuel the indefinite perpetuation of his vision. This can only be accomplished by the millions of us that are willing to take action today. We will only secure our rights by asserting them every single day of our lives.

Numerous black Americans spend a great part of life dealing with anger and the burden of discrimination. I tell my story to encourage those who follow to transform that anger and burden into a constructive force. The laws to protect us are in place but it is only by following through with the long, tedious process of deserved discrimination claims that these laws can serve us. Only when society is forced to pay the costs of mindless discrimination will its destructive results begin to be recognized. And only then will there begin to be less discrimination in the workplace.

Acknowledgments

To my wife, Norma, thanks for supporting my passion and sense of obligation to do this book. Her devotion and understanding helped me transform a dream, to a possibility, to a reality.

I owe a great debt to J.T. Dykman. Mr. Dykman provided sound editorial service and guidance that facilitated the completion of this book.

Finally, I would like to give special thanks to several people with whom I grew up. They provided invaluable information about their experiences as black youngsters growing up in Perth Amboy, NJ, during the 1940s and 1950s: Winston Hughes, Calvin Hughes, Cedric Richardson, Gail Cross, Bobby Leach, Betty Jane Dunn, Faye Maxwell Robinson, Louis Ruffin, Jane Handerson, Austin Gumbs, and the late Arthur Graham, Ernest Hazell and Joseph Davis, respectively.

CHAPTER ONE

Books are generally written about uncommon people. This is especially true of books about black Americans. The previous generation was the first in which black public figures gained national renown through books about exceptional achievers in fields such as the military, business, government, religion, sports, and human rights. We thank God for them and for the fact that our children have their stories to study and emulate.

As admirable as these leaders undoubtedly are, they are only a few of a racial heritage consisting of more than thirty million Americans. Who writes of the ordinary black man going about the business of raising a family and building a career in the face of all the obstacles a predominately white society still insists on placing in our path? I applaud our superstars as much as anyone else, but I also believe that true stories also need to be told about common people never wavering in the pursuit of justice. Discrimination in our nation will never end because of actions taken by those at the very top. It can only end when enough of us, probably measured in the millions, spend every day of our lives insisting on it.

My belief in pursuing justice came from my parents, Christopher and Helen Hughes. To understand how I could endure and prevail in the circumstances of my life, a little must be said about their lives.

They were born and raised to young adulthood on the island of Anguilla. It's just a speck on the map with a total land area less than a third of the size of Washington, D.C. Anguilla is one of the North Leeward Islands which demarcate the western end of the Atlantic

1

and the beginning of the Caribbean. In the 1920s, it was a desperately poor community. Many families depended on food and clothing regularly sent to them by relatives who had left the island. Although my father had become an expert carpenter at an early age and the house he built for his mother was a source of admiration, there was no work for him on a tiny island where the only sources of income were derived from fishing and salt export.

Anguilla is a British protectorate, which means it's not a nation, a dominion, or even a colony. The island was simply a place the British owned but never thought to nurture. It was impossible for young adults to believe that they or their children could have any future at all on what everyone called "The Rock." Emigration was the only option for most. Over many generations Anguillian communities emerged on the larger Caribbean islands, in various Latin American communities, in England, and in several American urban centers. My father made several attempts to earn a living without leaving home permanently. During the harvest season, he went to Cuba to cut sugarcane, and more than once he tried to find carpentry work on other islands. But tourists had not discovered the Caribbean in the 1920s and there were no construction projects on any of the islands in those days.

When my father came to the conclusion that his only hope for self-fulfillment required leaving "The Rock," he considered the matter with care. He chose the United States as his destination, because it seemed to be the only country where democracy and fairness prevailed. If there was any place that a poor West Indian had a chance to rise above the rigid caste systems of the Caribbean and Latin American societies, it had to be in America.

He chose Perth Amboy, NJ, because there was an active Anguillian community there as well as good prospects for employment. High on his list of reasons for going to Perth Amboy were the stories filtering back to relatives on "The Rock" that whites and blacks lived peacefully together there; all the discrimination laws everyone had heard about existed in states far to the south. He also chose Perth Amboy because of its picturesque waterfront and sailboating activities, akin to Anguilla's national pastime.

Perth Amboy was a town of heavy industry. There were smelters of ore, principally copper, silver and lead. It was a producer of asphalt, clay and steel. Large oil refineries lined the coasts. Most jobs required strong backs and people willing to work long hours in dirty, noisy and numbingly repetitive environments. It was, therefore, a town that attracted thousands of job-seeking immigrants. There were diverse communities of newcomers such as Poles, Ukrainians, Hungarians, Irish, Italians, Hispanics, and other Caucasian groups as well as blacks from the southern areas of America, Latin America and the Caribbean.

Dad's first encounter with injustice came when he was denied employment as a carpenter because the all-white unions would not accept black members at any level. The only work he could get was that of a pick-and-shovel laborer at Raritan Copper Works. Even at that level, however, he knew he could earn a living and he felt that future opportunities were possible. Neither of these notions could have applied to the situation in Anguilla.

The Sons and Daughters of Anguilla and the Anguilla Improvement Association were two organizations made up of first and second-generation West Indians living in Perth Amboy and surrounding communities. It was during one of their social events that my father and mother met each other. Before long they were in love and soon joined into a marriage that would last the rest of their lives.

My father was a strong man, both physically and mentally. As it turned out, he would never be allowed to join a union and rise above the level of laborer. He worked outside doing heavy lifting for the next 40 years. He was proud and some would say downright stubborn. Once he came to accept a belief, he no longer questioned it himself and seldom entertained the thoughts of those who did. He believed in discipline and rarely hesitated to wield his leather belt over the backside of any of his five sons who violated his code of conduct. He was intelligent. He never had a formal education, but always thirsted for knowledge and had the intellectual energy to pursue it. Dad read the newspapers every day and regularly engaged in serious conversations on world and local events. I doubt that there were many black laborers' children in Perth Amboy during those years whose fathers would carefully and often explain the philosophy of Mohandas Gandhi and how he was employing the concept of civil disobedience to free India from white British rule. Dad never doubted that this tiny pacifist, weighing less than ninety pounds, would eventually expel the world's largest colonial empire from his native land.

He also had a lyrical side and skillfully played the coronet, saxophone, guitar and accordion at home and at many local dances. He could not read music but only had to listen to a tune once to play

3

it faithfully from then on. Although he rarely praised my brothers and me in our presence and seldom explained himself or his decisions to us, he loved his family and spent his life doing his best for us. One of my most enduring memories is of Dad coming home in the evening drenched in sweat after an exhausting day. After cleaning up, he would then sit with us and discuss our day at school and our hopes for tomorrow.

Dad also demanded a deportment regimen from his children which we weren't allowed to question. We had to be in the house every night even though our friends would spend balmy summer evenings hanging out on the streets and in ice cream parlors. In the spring we would be the last children allowed to stop wearing sweaters and coats. We were poor, sometimes even desperate, but we rarely thought of ourselves as such.

Dad had a soft side that balanced his strictness. I remember him telling two of my older brothers to each give me twenty dollars for a high school graduation present. He would often take the family dog, Skippy, to the Dairy Queen to buy it an ice cream cone. Unbeknownst to us, he bragged about his five sons so much that Mom had to quiet him many times.

Mother had her own quiet pride and could discipline us, rarely raising her voice. Using a galvanized washboard, Mom did laundry every day. I still clearly remember my seventh grade teacher at the Samuel E. Shull School, a white lady named Mrs. Broadhead, expressing near amazement that the shirts I wore to school each day were bleached pure white and starched. She commented that my parents must really care about me. She was right. Even today I cannot leave the house without first inspecting my clothes to make sure everything is clean and correct.

Mother could sometimes mediate our punishments with Dad and, on many occasions, sure whippings could be reduced to less painful sanctions. Although I never saw it, she could become controlling if anything threatened the family itself. Years after the fact, my oldest brother, Calvin, told me that during the Depression, Dad was approached by friends who wanted him to run numbers in the Anguillian community. With the urgent need for money to support his family, Dad was about to agree when Mom put her tiny foot down and insisted he not take such a risk.

I am the youngest of five sons born to Helen and Christopher Hughes over a period of fourteen years after their marriage. First came Calvin, then Hilton, Christopher, Winston and myself. Since

4

Winston and I were nearest in age, we shared childhood closely together. Perth Amboy was not strictly segregated along racial or even ethnic lines in those days and there were many mixed neighborhoods. But Winston and I learned as we grew and explored that there were places to avoid. People of our color weren't welcome on High Street south of City Hall or in the several square blocks south of Market Street leading to the waterfront. We learned early on not to try hanging out at the Amboy Candy Kitchen, Texas Lunch, Coney Island Restaurant or the YMCA.

We had our own groups, such as the Sons and Daughters of Anguilla social club, where my mother and father had met, and the Anguilla Improvement Association, which held various events to raise money or collect old clothes for the folks still on "The Rock." Even small children were brought along to these gatherings and listened as the adults discussed life on the various islands and the way countries such as Great Britain, France, Holland and other nations of white Europe treated their Caribbean colonies and protectorates.

It was while eavesdropping on these adult discussions that I got my first sense of my father's inclinations toward racial fairness. The Improvement Association had the word Anguilla as its name, but many members from other Caribbean islands such as Dominica, St. Marten and St. Vincent were also admitted. Since the social events and the activities of gathering canned goods and clothes to send home were always occasions for both fun and intelligent discussion, black immigrants from other places frequently tried to join. My father felt that any well-intentioned black person should be granted membership. A lifelong member of the National Association for the Advancement of Colored People, Dad felt that any group of blacks should be as inclusive as possible. He often pointed out his belief that discrimination by Anguillians against other blacks was every bit as bad as white discrimination against all of us. The majority of the Anguillia Improvement Association felt otherwise, however, and Dad was consistently voted down. Listening to his arguments at these meetings gave my brothers and me our first understanding of the need for racial solidarity.

Calvin and Winston both wanted music as the central aspect of their lives. By the time I was in first grade, Calvin was an adult and already on the road traveling with various jazz bands. Since Winston and I were close, I knew that the one thing he wanted most was to become a member of the Flagstaff Drum and Bugle Corps.

The all-black Drum and Bugle Corps had been founded by the

Flagstaff Foods Company because the local Lions Club Drum and Bugle Corps would not admit blacks. We all had deep pride in our corps and I still remember, as a very small child, marching along the sidewalk trying to keep up with the Flagstaff Corps. The organization competed in and won awards in parades up and down the Mid-Atlantic states. By the time Winston was old enough to join, he believed he could play drums in the band, especially since he already knew all their tunes. But every time he asked permission our father refused to let him join. This became the major disappointment in Winston's adolescent life. Dad's refusal was based on his own misguided perception of what was best for Winston's future in music.

My father's own well-known musical ability came about because he could play by ear. Since the Flagstaff Drum and Bugle Corps had no music instructors, everything the organization played depended on the ability of its members to learn and act by hearing rather than by written instruction. Dad already had Calvin playing the trumpet and reading music and he wanted Winston to also read music. Dad wanted more for him and had arranged for Winston to take private piano lessons during which he was taught to read music. Dad believed that if Winston joined the Drum and Bugle Corps he would not learn music the proper way. In fact, he was convinced, incorrectly, that continuing to learn music by ear would somehow harm Winston's ability to learn to read and follow sheet music. Our father's intentions were founded on love and his aspirations for his son to rise above his contemporaries. But it was a long time before we understood.

Just after the end of World War II, Dad experienced an accident at work that changed his life. Crude copper ore from South America was shipped to Raritan Copper Works and mixed with pure copper in large tanks. The mixture was then poured into large iron molds for further processing. One of the heavy molds slipped while Dad was filling it and the fingers on his left hand were damaged. Most of his ring finger had to be amputated. Pain killers were not readily available in those days and narcotics such as morphine were reserved for life-threatening injuries. So, Dad experienced continuous and serious discomfort during the year it took for his hand to heal enough for him to use a shovel again. Raritan Copper Works offered no assistance and the accident insurance policy that Dad had been paying for every month for years (which included a dismemberment clause) was not honored by the company that issued it. Mother worked days and weekends at the local skating rink to get us through this troubling time. The saddest legacy of the accident was that Dad could never again play his favorite instruments, the hand accordion and the guitar.

Dad was always on alert for ways to improve life for his family. In the spring of 1947, he noticed a three-story brick house for sale in a predominately white neighborhood of Polish and Ukrainian immigrants. Moving to this house would have been, by itself, a substantial increase in the quality of our family life. But my father was attracted to it mainly as a business opportunity. The three-story structure had been converted into a three-unit apartment building with a storefront, then being used by a white tenant who was also a preacher.

Knowing the neighborhood, the owner and the tenants were white, Dad recognized that he would be rejected if he openly sought to buy the place. My father never feared whites and deeply hated their discrimination; but he also understood how to deal with the system. He had a white friend go with him to inspect the property and pretend to be the prospective buyer, while my father went along posing as a carpenter who might be hired to make renovations for the buyer. After protracted third-party negotiations, Dad purchased the house and was able to qualify for a mortgage based on his many years of perfect rent payments. For the first time, our family had its own bathroom, rather than having to share with other tenants.

We occupied the middle floor and the tenants lived on the third and first floors. The white renters on the third floor were outraged that a black person had bought into the neighborhood and they resented having to pay rent to a person of color. Dad never took their verbal abuse without an equally loud retort and kept suggesting to them that they relocate to a place where they would be more comfortable. After months of arguments, the family finally left. Dad immediately rented the apartment to a friendly black family. The white tenants on the first floor were the opposite of those on the top floor and we had friendly relations with them from the outset.

The most important change came about a year later when the preacher and his family moved out in order to reside in a place that would accommodate a larger church. Dad then rebuilt the front of the building into a confectionery store and soda fountain and renovated the rear space into a small rental unit. We ran the storefront and sold staples like bread and milk, newspapers, candy and cigarettes. We even had a nickel jukebox. The main money-maker was the soda fountain where Winston and I concocted many locally famous dishes made up of ice cream, fruit and sauces.

The store became a family enterprise. Mother would operate it in the mornings and early afternoons. When Winston and I came home from school we would take over and Dad would handle the evening trade while we did our homework. As we grew and entered high school, we became increasingly less enchanted with working every day in the store because important things like baseball, basketball and social events were becoming available to us. We knew better than to suggest to our father the idea of our abandoning the business for activities he would regard as frivolous. Our solution was to divide the work among ourselves by working on alternate days instead of together every day. If we had asked permission, I'm not sure what Dad's answer would have been. But when he found out what we were doing, he was proud that we had worked it out amongst ourselves. Although we couldn't see it at the time, our working in the store met one of Dad's goals for us: we learned how to deal with all sorts of people and gained the pride of representing the family in the business.

Just when I began high school, the Dairy Queen company built a store across the street from us and thereby put our little confection operation out of business. Undaunted, my father rebuilt the front area into rooms for transients and the place remained a rooming house for many more years.

Perth Amboy High School was a mixed experience for black Americans. We represented about 10 percent of the student body; while there was little overt or systemic discrimination, there were subtle clouds of it throughout my experience. Nobody ever said we were not allowed to attend school dances, but when we did attend we were made to feel uncomfortable. There were no rules against black cheerleaders; there just were too few. At the same time, many black youths did well at school. I remember that Austin Gumbs was president of both his junior and senior classes, while his brother Franklin was president of his class. David Rey and Cedric Richardson became presidents of their classes as well. To our parents' joy, my brother Winston was elected by the student body to be "Mayor of Perth Amboy" and got to run the city for a day.

What happened on the athletic fields was almost totally dependent upon the coach of each sport. The football and basketball teams had few black players. Even on the rare occasions when

8

a black student made the team, he spent the games warming the bench. Track and field, however, was coached by a Jewish man named Leo Klein who never excluded any student willing to make an honest effort to succeed. The natural consequence of this inclusiveness was that it became the sport which attracted black athletes. Coach Klein's teams won tournaments and black youth under his guidance were awarded college scholarships. At the same time the track team was considered respectable, our basketball team concluded its season with a record of five wins and eighteen losses, while Cedric Hodge, a black athlete capable of scoring twenty points a game, rarely was allowed off the bench.

Academic advancement was left to the individual black student without any hindrance or support from the white staff or teachers. My grades were mediocre during my first two years but became better in my junior and senior years. No counselor or teacher ever encouraged me or even thought to mention the possibility of college. In addition to being president of our senior class, Cedric Richardson was a good athlete, an honors scholar and a leader in school activities. He told me that his counselor was visibly shocked when he mentioned wanting to go on to college. On his own, he got to Seton Hall University and became a renowned public school educator during his distinguished career.

Early in my high school days, I discovered a natural skill at playing billiards and it became a lifelong competitive activity. Our hometown pool expert at that time was Steve Mizerak Sr., whose son, Steve Mizerak Jr., would later become a World Straight Pool and Nine-Ball Champion. Steve Jr. and I played regularly during those years and both he and his father, a New Jersey Straight Pool Champion himself, taught me invaluable pool techniques and strategies.

Neither Steve nor his father taught me humility; I had to learn that on my own. One morning Dad gave me a twenty-dollar bill and instructed me to return the change after getting a haircut. I walked out of the barbershop with Dad's $18.50 in my pocket and headed straight for Mizerak's pool room, confident that I could double it. I engaged in a series of nine-ball games against an opponent I knew I could beat. I was so scared of losing my Dad's money that I couldn't keep my concentration and managed to lose all of it. In 1954, $18.50 was important to Dad, and the loss of it was terrifying to me. The next morning, my mother asked Dad for some money and he sent her to me for his $18.50. I knew I was in deep trouble. When

9

she asked me for it, I immediately blurted out a dumb lie that I had lost it at the movies. Dad overheard us and knew I was lying. Out came the razor strap and only my mother's pleas stopped him after several heavy strokes. I had already known better than to lie to my parents. The real lesson I learned from the experience was to never play scared.

Despite the selective exclusions of some aspects of the experience, I recall my years of growing up and graduating from high school in Perth Amboy as, essentially, happy ones. We never had pocket money, cars, out-of-town vacations, and other things that our white friends routinely enjoyed. But we never thought of our family as disadvantaged or any less fulfilling than anyone else's. Our store closed just as I entered high school and I took on many jobs to earn money and help the family. I shined shoes downtown, delivered groceries for Davidson's Fruit and Vegetable Company, delivered *The Newark Star Ledger* newspaper for three years and worked with my Uncle Fanny on his produce truck. Each job was good for me and I took something positive away from each one. In all cases, the customers I worked for were predominately white and there never seemed to be any lack of respect. I grew up thinking that racially mixed neighborhoods were the way things should be. Two of my best white friends, Louis Arce and Kenny Chordas, were also good friends with my two best black friends, Ernie Hazell and Bobby Davis.

Almost every black youth who has grown up in America did so in an environment of racial discrimination. But in my early experiences, it was never as pervasive or as mean-spirited as that which I would encounter later. We had our own role models. The earliest in my memory was Joe Louis, the former World Heavyweight Champion. I'll never forget the time Dad took me to Pompton Lakes, NJ, to watch him in training. One of our greatest heroes, Jackie Robinson, the first African-American to play baseball in the major leagues, routinely endured racial taunts from white players and fans; yet he always maintained his dignity, never retaliated, and he excelled. His public demeanor was a great part of what made us so proud. We also had our local leaders who made us proud. Herbert Richardson became Perth Amboy's first black teacher in 1949. Milton Campbell, from nearby Plainfield, NJ, was our sports hero in high school, especially so later on when he was a decathlon medalist in the 1952 and 1956 World Olympics. Closer to home, our family was always proud of Calvin, who played the trumpet

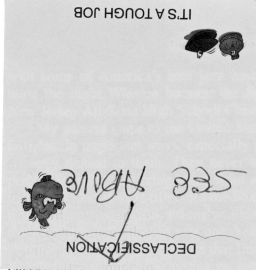

cians. Our buttons nearly
st black conductor of the
us.

es in hope of freedom and
n employment, it was per-
topped trying or lost their
chool forms for my parents
marked "occupation" with
't let him engage in it, but
rs later, after he passed on,
used while taking English
classes after coming to... t people wouldn't think he
was uneducated. Tears welled within me as I leafed through them.
I could visualize this strong man striving hard to educate himself
despite working as a laborer. My parents gave their sons life principles to guide us. Perhaps the strongest one they gave me was to
never countenance unfair treatment so long as there was any way to
oppose it.

11

Eric's Father, Christopher Hughes, at 35 years of age

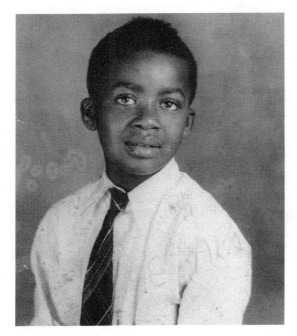

Eric Hughes — 8 years old

Eric Hughes at 14 years old and the late Arthur Graham

Eric Hughes
Perth Amboy High School — 15 years old

Eric Hughes
2nd row, 2nd from the right
Perth Amboy High School — 15 years old

Eric Hughes
Perth Amboy High School — 17 years old

Eric Hughes
Perth Amboy High School — 18 years old

Eric Hughes and Mother on her 84th birthday

CHAPTER TWO

Even though the war in Korea had been over for three years when I graduated from high school, the military draft remained a universal aspect in the life of every young American man for another generation. In addition to my diploma, I also had a draft card with a 1-A classification. Since I was neither married nor on my way to college, the chances of being drafted into military service were high indeed. Beyond this fact of life was the youthful feeling of wishing to see and experience more of the world than had been available to me in Perth Amboy. I chose to enlist in the United States Air Force and thereby began what would become a lifetime of public service in the federal government.

Even though black Americans had fought and died in military service to their country for almost two hundred years, less than seven years had elapsed since President Truman had ordered complete desegregation in all branches of the military. It would be another ten years before the first federal civil rights laws would begin to enforce racial integration in civilian society. So the military was then the only group within our nation that required its members to work together without racial discrimination. Without the slightest knowledge of it, I thereby became a part of what would become a sea of change in our country's national life.

It was a hot June day in 1955 when I arrived at Sampson Air Force Base in Geneva, NY, for basic training. Our training unit, Flight 4429, was made up of 60 young men from Virginia, West Virginia and New Jersey. That day was my first experience with whites who hated me on sight. In Perth Amboy, I knew white people who didn't like blacks and had experienced all the forms of discrimination American blacks routinely encountered in a white society. But I had never faced a stranger who expressed clear animosity at the prospect of being forced to stand next to me. Other white recruits, whom I would later learn shared this deep prejudice, kept their feelings to themselves whenever possible. Some of the rest evidenced pure curiosity since they had never before been in the same room with a black person or actually spoken to one.

There were relatively few racial skirmishes during basic training because, in my opinion, we were simply too exhausted by the intense physical regimen. The instructors never gave us a chance to get into serious trouble; our days were filled with close order drill, physical training, obstacle courses and tightly controlled classroom exercises. We were never allowed to walk anywhere. The only permissible paces were either a fast jog or flat out run. By the end of each day we were just too tired for anything except sack time. Many of our initial group, who had joined the Air Force in the mistaken belief that the training would be softer than the Army or Navy, dropped out during basic because they just couldn't take it.

Toward the end of our initial training we were given a series of aptitude and skill tests to determine what occupations might be best for us to enter while in the service. I scored well in language comprehension and manual dexterity and was therefore assigned to Francis E. Warren Air Force Base in Cheyenne, WY, to learn the military teletype system. During the next four months, I learned to typewrite with a teletype machine, to read perforated tape and to master all the protocols connected with formatting, sending, and receiving military telegraphic messages. I enjoyed the course and did well. To be at the center of Air Force communications seemed an exciting prospect. The minimum speed to graduate was 25 words per minute. By the end of the course, I could do double that requirement. After scoring very near the top in our final exams, I joined an elite group selected to go on to military cryptographic school at Scott Air Force Base.

Scott was located near the town of Belleville, IL, about 40 miles south of St. Louis. I threw myself into the course and found the idea of being entrusted with secret communications exciting. Encrypting and decrypting telegrams, many of which were top secret, gave us a sense of genuine importance. The mechanics of cryptography came easily to me and I became one of the fastest cryptographers in my class. A good part of the course was given over to security. Executing secret communications was only half of the subject material. The other half was being taught to protect the secrets we were to handle. We were trained to not let slip any hint of message content no matter how casual a conversation we might be having and no matter with whom we might be having it. Heady stuff for a youngster, but I never heard of anyone violating communications security during or after our training.

The town of Belleville was the nearest place for us to go during the first day we were allowed off base and I joined a group of friends on the way there for whatever entertainment we might find. It was an awful awakening for me.

We were denied entrance to the movie theater and to other public establishments. For the first time, I saw signs in businesses that read, "We Do Not Serve Negroes." In the tiny central park, there were dual drinking fountains with one labeled, "For Whites Only." There had been nothing like this in Perth Amboy. This was our welcome to the land of Lincoln. No number of passing years will ever dim my memories of pain and rage at these rejections of my humanity because of my skin color.

After completing my cryptographic training, I received (with considerable joy) my assignment to Norton Air Force Base outside of San Bernardino, CA. It was not the prospect of streets lined with palm trees nor the famous clement weather that made the assignment so attractive to me; it was the reputation of Southern California as a laid back lifestyle, free of blatantly enforced segregation.

As I applied my new skills to live telegrams at Norton, I quickly made new friends and was invited to join the base basketball team. It was a very good team and my skills at the game improved markedly as I strove to keep up with the better players. During my tenure there, the team won several championships. When I went home on leave and joined my old friends in pickup games, they all remarked on my new sharpness at the game. Cryptography was then a vocation that required complete and close concentration during every step. No one could stay at it for too many hours without losing some level of concentration. For this reason, our work shifts were shorter than normal. With extra time on my hands, I made serious work at the billiard table and used my winnings to buy an eight-year-old Mercury. California was meeting my expectations.

One of my fellow cryptographers was a young, white woman from Lake Charles, LA, named Barbara. Sometimes we worked the graveyard shift together and since things at the communications center became slow after midnight, we talked and got to know each other. Being from the deep south, Barbara had been raised in an atmosphere of racism and I was the first black person with whom she had ever held a conversation. We candidly discussed race relations with each other and I soon learned that the prejudices taught by her mother had not taken firm root. Before long, we could converse in a friendly and honest manner.

One afternoon, I was playing in a softball game which Barbara attended. As the sun went down, the air became cooler and she asked to borrow my high school jacket. As soon as she put it on, the atmosphere changed. There were hard stares at me from my teammates and the people seated around Barbara stopped talking with her. Later on she told me how shocked she had been by the sudden silent hostility from those who had been so friendly only a moment previously. I tried to explain to her that I had not been the least bit shocked. Later on, I walked with her around the base after we left the communications center. We were simply two friends talking about life and fairly oblivious to the rest of the world. There was never anything between us except a casual friendship and, in fact, her boyfriend, Bob, was also a friend of mine and a member of my basketball team. When Barbara got back to her dormitory, she received several phone calls from female friends advising her not to be seen alone in public with a black man. The next day, Bob told me he intended to marry Barbara and then asked me to leave her alone. She and I remained friendly, but we never spoke alone in public again and I stopped regarding Bob as my friend.

My next assignment was to Rothweston Air Force Station at Kassel in central Germany. There I learned that white Americans held no patents on racial discrimination. It was my first experience watching white people cross the street to avoid having to share a sidewalk with blacks. There were no placards refusing service to Negroes, but I was frequently refused service in sidewalk cafes and restaurants while white soldiers and airmen were happily eating and drinking.

I arrived in Germany just as the 1957 racial crisis was coming to a flashpoint in Little Rock, AR. Headlines everywhere showed Governor Faubus standing at the door to the local high school, denying entrance to a little, black girl. President Eisenhower sent federal troops to keep order. My country could applaud the black All-American basketball star Oscar Robertson at the University of

Cincinnati, while at the same time requiring military force to allow black students to attend a southern high school.

Probably because of the publicized racial tensions at home, extra efforts were made on military bases to maintain orderly racial relationships while on duty. It was only off-base that the true feelings of many white servicemen became starkly evident. German girls told me that white soldiers frequently lectured them to stay away from black personnel because they all had horrible diseases, tails like monkeys and were constantly dirty. Fights would burst out spontaneously whenever a black serviceman would dance with a white, German woman.

The depth of white, racial hatred usually bared itself after ingestion of substantial amounts of alcohol. Almost every time, on the bus back to base after a night on the town, some drunken whites would start shouting racial epithets or loudly tell each other so-called jokes about Negroes. By that time we would be in no mood to put up with it and a fistfight would erupt. Usually such brawls generated only superficial wounds, but it was a rare event when the last bus to the base arrived without blood on the floor and seats.

My time in Germany was not completely ruined by the extracurricular racial environment. Being a cryptographer, I had extra time on my hands and resumed my billiard activity. I won the base elimination tournament, which earned me the right to represent Rothweston in the pool championship where Air Force base winners from all over Germany came to compete. Placing third in that tournament gave me something of a reputation and I played many exhibition games around Germany with Frank McGowan, who became both a European and a New York State Straight Pool Champion.

During my service there, I also became friends with a white airman named Richard Underwood. We used to take long rides through rural German towns in his Volkswagen for no better reason than to enjoy the scenery and listen to jazz on the radio. Richard was an excellent clarinet player, and I often joined him in impromptu jam sessions with German musicians at the local airman's club. I played the congas and bongo drums but wanted to try a wind instrument. Richard talked me into spending three hundred dollars, which I had won in a dice game, on a brand new flute. Under his coaching, I became fairly good with it and joined in playing old American standards during the sessions.

Several times, our wanderings in Richard's Volkswagen took

us to Copenhagen. We did all the tourist things such as introducing ourselves to the little mermaid and visiting Tivoli Gardens, but the thing that struck me about Denmark was the friendliness of the people. In complete contrast to the burghers of Germany, the Danes welcomed conversations with black servicemen and I never once saw the instinctive white reaction to treat blacks as something less than equals. Richard and I remained friends long after we left military service.

I had other white friends in addition to Richard, but there were usually unintended aspects to the relationship. For instance, I had a white friend named Sam with whom I had worked for several months. Once, Sam and I were detailed to pick up some materials in a truck and were driving across the base when I saw a group of airmen running across a field on the base. I said, "Who the hell are those guys, and why are they running?" Immediately Sam replied, "Oh, they're just a bunch of niggers." I was shocked because it never occurred to me that Sam would use such a word and he was profoundly mortified at having said it. He spent the rest of the trip apologizing and doing his best to express remorse at having made the comment. Somehow, he tried to explain, he had become so comfortable around me that he didn't even think of me as a black person and the epithet had just come out without his thinking. We remained friendly for the remainder of our tour of duty, but we were no longer friends.

My military service drew to a close after my assignment overseas. Many aspects of being in the Air Force had been good for me. I learned the meaning of responsibility and this would serve me well later on during my years of civilian government service. I acquired high skill levels in the fields of telemetry and cryptography. Concepts such as a solid work ethic and team leadership became comfortable for me. Most importantly, I gathered confidence in my own abilities. Although several officers did their best in trying to talk me into remaining in the Air Force, I had reached the conclusion that a military career was not for me. I wanted more freedom and I especially wanted to be able to choose where I lived. In addition, I had begun to think about college and in those days you couldn't earn scholarships by re-enlistment.

Eric Hughes — Sampson AFB, New York

Eric Hughes, 2nd row, 2nd from left —
graduation from Teletype school, Cheyenne, Wyoming

Norton AFB, California — Eric Hughes, 1st on right

Norton AFB, California — Eric Hughes, 1st on right

Eric Hughes — Copenhagen, Denmark

Frank McGowan, Eric Hughes and Melvin Joseph —
billiards tournament in Germany

CHAPTER THREE

Upon leaving the Air Force, I went home to Perth Amboy. As much as I loved my hometown and valued my many friends there, my experiences and travels during military service had introduced me to a much wider world. For the first time, I knew what I wanted in life: to go to school, earn a degree, get a good job, become self sufficient, start fresh in a new environment and meet new people. Since my four-year grade point average in high school was less than outstanding, college scholarships didn't seem possible. I decided to concentrate, first, on finding a job in the city where I wanted to live and then explore ways to go to school while working fulltime.

Even before leaving the service, I had decided that I wanted to work for the federal government and I'd heard a lot about Washington, D.C. At the time, I read national African-American magazines such as *Ebony* and *Jet* and it seemed to me that all the action was centered in our nation's capital. As soon as I got home I began filling out federal employment applications and sending them to Washington.

My only apprehension was in moving south. The civil rights movement had begun to gain national visibility by the late 1950s and stories of white retaliation in the southern United States were beginning to receive national attention. The case of Emmet Till, which I'll never forget, was in the headlines. Till was a black teenager from Chicago who was visiting family in Mississippi when he was attacked by a mob for allegedly whistling at a white woman. They beat him savagely, tied a chain around his neck, attached a concrete block to it and threw him in the river. This senseless and brutal killing enraged all black communities around the country and such vicious retaliation for so slight an offense gave pause to anyone of color who was considering moving south. Would Washington be like Belleville, IL?

But my goal was to work for the U.S. government, and Washington was its heart. So I continued sending applications and hoped for the best.

The day I received a letter from the U.S. Department of State was one of my happiest. It contained a job offer for a crypto-graphic/teletype position at its Washington headquarters. At the time, I didn't really understand what a GS-4 job level meant, but I surely understood what a salary of $3,770 meant in early 1960. It doesn't seem like much money today, but 40 years ago, such a sum was a starting salary a young man could be proud of. I spent the day going around my hometown telling the good news to all my friends. My parents, who understood how much I wanted to join the federal workforce, were particularly happy and proud.

When I arrived in Washington in February of 1960, I didn't know a soul, but I was indeed fortunate to be taken in by close friends of my sister-in-law. These good people invited me into their lovely home and graciously helped me as I started my job and explored the city. To this day I have kept in touch with this gener-ous family.

In 1960, Washington had a population of about eight hundred thousand, which made it almost twenty times larger than Perth Amboy. I felt as if I knew almost everyone in my native New Jersey town, but all the people in Washington, D.C. were strangers. It was almost overwhelming for a young black man who had grown up in a city with about a ten percent minority population to suddenly find himself in a large metropolitan city where the vast majority of the population was of his own race. Where I came from, almost every trade or professional person was white. But in Washington, the peo-ple engaged in everything from shoemaking to store ownership. Attorneys, insurance brokers, city officials, judges, dentists, and doctors were of African heritage. Just being in a city where the majority of professionals, in and out of government, were predom-inately of my race made me glad and proud.

My introduction to the nation's capital was made smooth and enriched by being taken into the home of Ed and Beulah "Shug" Blevins. My sister-in-law, Betty Hughes, had grown up with Shug and had arranged for me to stay with them when I arrived in the city. They welcomed me warmly and, in a sense, became my surrogate parents during my early months. Ed was an employee of the State Department and gave me good counseling concerning the political and racial aspects of both the department and the city. It took him decades to break through the ingrained discrimination within the department. But before retiring in 1987, Ed Blevins managed to become one of the highest African-American professionals in department history. Shug exercised all her maternal instincts toward me from the moment I crossed their threshold in 1960. She kept an immaculate home. By working as a counselor at a home for delinquent children, Boys Village in Cheltenham, MD. Shug contributed to their income sufficiently to furnish their home in a style I had not previously experienced. Ed passed away shortly after retiring. Shug Blevins and I remain in touch today and we've never lost the feeling of being family.

It didn't take me long to affirm my decision to come to Washington. The young people who became my new friends seemed to have the same optimism and aspirations I had. Our conversations centered around starting or finishing college and advancing in worthwhile careers. I had always leaned toward higher education and these talks strongly reinforced my intent. It was thrilling to be in such an environment.

My start at the Department of State, which I soon learned was called simply "State" by everyone in Washington, was a time of happy beginnings. The communications center received and transmitted encoded telegrams from and to more than 300 embassies, consulates and outposts worldwide. No one had computers in those days and we had to use teletype or cryptographic machines to manually type each character of every word, sentence and paragraph of those telegrams, many of which were more than 30 pages of single-spaced typing. I was an efficient typist at 75 words per minute and worked hard to master all the teletype procedures and systems.

Work in the communications center gave me a feeling of making a genuine contribution. It was at a time when nations from all over Africa were fighting for independence. The war in Vietnam was not yet escalating, but diplomatic telegraphic traffic was heavy. Important messages were pouring into State and responses to them had to be encoded and sent out quickly. The center was a 24-hour operation and, being a newcomer, I worked at night. I came to feel that I was a vital part of the center's mission. During the early years I received timely promotions and believed I was at the outset of a rewarding career.

There were a few civilian-trained women working in the center. Almost all the employees were former military men, causing the racial composition to be about evenly split between whites and blacks.

It wasn't hard to notice, however, that outside the communications center there was a different situation in the department. The few black employees were almost universally in the lowest paying jobs, such as messengers who distributed telegrams and mail from office to office. These positions were all at the GS-1 or GS-2 level. At first I was glad that my military experience had earned me entrance at the GS-4 level.

In 1963, my father lost a three-year fight with cancer and died. I returned to Perth Amboy for the funeral and, for the first time, my brothers and I sat around openly talking with each other about our Dad. Calvin, being the oldest, told stories some of us hadn't heard before about the rent parties Anguillians would hold for each other during the Depression and how Dad positioned him at the door to collect the coins as people arrived at the party. We all laughed at his story about the time Dad had been cutting sugarcane in Cuba and a fellow worker sat on what he thought to be a log and then ran away upon discovering that it was a huge snake. The man was never seen again. Calvin told us how one day Dad went looking for a white man who had harassed Mom and Aunt Eliza at the movies and we laughed about what the outcome would have been had he found the man. One time Calvin needed his band uniform and discovered the owner had closed his store early. Calvin told Dad, who convinced the owner to give Calvin his uniform. Calvin related that he had neglected to write home for months and Dad rode a train from Perth Amboy to Dayton, OH, to find out about his son's welfare. Each of us had our own tales to recount and all of them added up to the many strengths our father had possessed and tried to pass to us in his own, often obscure, way. We all shared the sadness that, with the exception of Calvin, none of us had ever really talked with him about life itself.

Perhaps it was part of my continuing remorse over Dad's racially restricted life and his recent passing, but after returning to work it became increasingly clear to me that blacks were rarely, if ever, awarded good paying jobs in the early sixties. The only genuine promotional track at State was occupied by white, male Ivy League graduates. They were the ones who were appointed to the elite Foreign Service Institute and training there was requisite for promotions and overseas assignments.

The personnel system itself was set up in a way to assure such results. The system was headed by a director general who was putatively responsible for human resource recruitment, training and development throughout the department. In fact, however, the director general maintained direct and personal responsibility for the Foreign Service system and had a subordinate manager in charge of domestic employees. It was a transparent structure which let everyone see that anyone not hired for Foreign Service was somehow less important. When you added to this situation the fact that, outside of the communications center there were almost no blacks above the grade of GS-2, it was easy to see who was riding in the back of the bus.

These were the days when civil rights legislation, which would create institutions such as the Equal Employment Opportunity Commission, was being debated in Congress but had not yet become law. Difficult as it was for me to live with such unfairness, I kept believing that continued hard work and high-quality output would eventually lead to advancement.

While the work itself was interesting, this schedule of working on the night shift prevented me from exploring the social life in my newly adopted city. It was difficult to make new friends outside of the communications center since I would be on my way to work at the hour when everyone else was leaving their jobs to socialize. Having Ed and Shug Blevins as friends and mentors helped in dealing with my sense of loneliness.

Finally, late in 1963, I had earned my way to the day shift and could take up the life of a normal person. The Washington social life available to a single young man was full indeed. Before long I had joined local sports teams and began playing baseball and basketball again. There were numerous black entertainment clubs in those days and I soon introduced myself to the Flamingo, Chez Maurice, Birdland and Pat & GG's. Some of the best hotels held cabarets where we would dress up and spend the evening dancing and enjoying floorshows. My circle of friends grew rapidly, and many of the young men I hung out with in the sixties have remained in touch over three decades.

In November 1966, while with a group of friends at a Washington cabaret, I was introduced to a beautiful woman named Norma Jean Tibbs. A native of Washington, she was employed at the U.S. Department of Interior. Intelligent, sophisticated and possessing a generous spirit toward others, Norma became the center of my life from that day forward. We were married in August of 1968 and are as committed to each other today as we were on that lovely summer day 34 years ago. Our union included Norma's seven-year-old daughter, Tracy. Wendy, our second daughter, was born two years later.

In June 1970, I enrolled in the University of the District of Columbia and was able to arrange my courses around a changing work schedule. My hope was that a degree would make it impossible for management to continue overlooking me.

Another two years passed without a promotion (still GS-8). I was beginning to despair about my future, when I was called into my supervisor's office. They informed me that a new office was going to be opened to handle certain highly classified and sensitive communications and they had selected me to research the complex problems and procedures involved in setting it up. They let me know that I was being offered the position at the GS-9 level (with the understanding that the position would go to GS-11) because I had the experience and had proven that I was both dependable and trustworthy.

Nothing could have been more timely or made me happier. I still remember the joyful look on my wife's face when I told her about it. She knew how hard I had worked hoping that a break like this would happen. We celebrated my promotion by going to dinner and discussing our happiness about my new opportunity.

The new position allowed me entrance to the management side of communications. Now I could work with the officials who actually sent and received the telegrams and I would have a much broader view of department goals and objectives. Since the job had no written operating procedures, I was free to develop them as I went along. Where support positions complemented one another and the new office, I drafted new procedures for them as well. I gave my all to the tasks at hand. I worked when a severe cold should have had me home in bed and I lost weeks of vacation because I wouldn't take the time off. I was serious about my work and I enjoyed it. I finally had the chance to demonstrate leadership. I received the highest possible performance rating, "outstanding," during each of the four appraisal periods I worked on the project.

When everything was completed, I handed my supervisors the finished manual of operating procedures. They told me that I had received high praise from the managers I had been working with and they appreciated the fact that several of the performance standards I had developed were going to be instituted for all employees in the section. It seemed to be general knowledge in the office that I had earned a grade-promotion to take over the new position permanently.

To my shock, the director of the communications center ignored the recommendations of my supervisors and promoted another employee to the permanent position. The director was a white man and the person he appointed was a black woman who had no knowledge concerning the work involved.

Word of her promotion spread quickly throughout the office. Both my supervisors and co-workers went out of their way to tell me how sorry they were that I had been treated unfairly. Even though they were embarrassed and awkward about the situation, my supervisors had to be very careful because everyone knew that Ben, the director of communications, was the type of manager who would undercut them for even minor provocations.

My supervisors also were concerned about the effects of Ben's decision on my attitude and morale. They were correct in this concern. If I had been on a roller coaster, this was the lowest point. Frustration and long-suppressed anger had begun to get the best of me. I had problems eating and lost weight. Even family members were telling me I was hard to get along with.

Before long, however, I was able to restore equilibrium with nothing more than the willpower my parents had given me by example when unfairness had upset their lives during my childhood. I still had enormous pride and I would not have it destroyed. I recognized that I had earned the respect of my co-workers, my supervisors and managers in other agencies. I was not going to throw these relationships away because of one person's discriminatory action.

I was not going to lie down either. By this time, there were federal Equal Employment Opportunity procedures and State had a brand new Office of Civil Rights.

My first action was to personally confront Ben and I demanded a meeting. He was a former Central Intelligence Agency manager and tried his best during the meeting to avoid stating a reason for not promoting me. He tried to sell me the old horse about competition getting stiffer the higher you go, but I wasn't buying. I met with him two additional times and he failed on both occasions to give me any logical reason for promoting a person devoid of experience over me. Although he was smart enough not to say it outright, I got the firm impression that he was not disposed to promote black men. He did let slip the notion that his action achieved two of the new minority requirements in that the person he appointed was both black and female. His attitude gave me the impression that he felt smug in his position since he assumed that I couldn't claim discrimination about another black worker being promoted over me.

My wife and I discussed these events at some length because any action I might take could seriously affect my career and, therefore, my family. On the other hand, it was obvious I had genuine problems dealing with my anger. We talked about the job enrichment I had gained from the recent effort and my dedication to the center. We also explored the fact that the recently passed equal opportunity laws were being implemented, but no one knew for sure how things might work out if I tried using them. In the end, we both agreed that I could not let it pass.

The first step in the process of filing a federal discrimination complaint requires the concerned agency (in my case State) to assign an Equal Employment Opportunity counselor to try to resolve the matter before a formal complaint is filed. A counselor was assigned to my case and interviewed several managers as well as employees. Everyone he talked to believed that I should have been awarded the position. He also reviewed my performance ratings and verified that I had received outstanding appraisals every year. He could find no reason why I should not have been promoted. His findings also revealed that, while my complaint was not justified on the basis of racial discrimination, the person promoted over me having been black, it was justified on the merits alone.

Both the counselor and the Office of Communications personnel officer recommended to Ben that I be promoted to the position. They pointed out that if he did not resolve the situation, I was going to go ahead with a formal complaint that could bring him a lot of trouble. Ben agreed with them in theory, but his problem was that the black woman he had promoted now held the only available GS-11 position in the section. The only action he could now take was to promote me to the GS-10 position that became open due to the promotion of the black woman to the position I was claiming.

When I was offered this compromise I hesitated for a couple of days to make up my mind. While it was indeed a promotion, it certainly wasn't the one I was convinced I deserved. It would also involve my return to nightshift work, which would disrupt both my family life and my college schedule. There comes a point, however, when it just seems best to get on with life, and I accepted their offer.

Just after this disappointment, I found reason for joy when Interior's Department of Fisheries merged with the National Oceanic and Atmospheric Administration and my wife was selected for the Upward Mobility Program with a target position of personnel management specialist.

CHAPTER FOUR

My new position as a communications supervisor gave me eligibility to take courses at the Foreign Service Institute, as long as they were related to my official duties. I took them not only to improve my management skills but also to provide evidence of my commitment to the goals and objectives of the department. My aim was to do everything I could, on the job and in college, to show my dedication to be the best possible employee. At the same time, I became more dedicated than ever to earning my degree because I believed it would materially assist me in seeking other career opportunities.

About four months after accepting the compromise, an unexpected vacancy opened and I was able to return to the day shift in the same position of communications supervisor. The change made life much easier for my family since we were able to see each other during the week. It also boosted my morale because I was able to rejoin my many friends in the center and throughout the department.

The most important consequence of resuming work during daylight hours was the ability to readjust my college schedule. Most of the remaining courses I needed for my degree were offered at night and I could now get back into a full academic program. The result was that I was awarded a bachelor's degree in community planning and development in 1974.

The year 1974 also yielded one of my proudest moments at State when I was selected to provide communications support to the White House for President Nixon's third summit meeting at Yalta with Russia's Communist Party leader Leonid Brezhnev and Secretary of State Henry Kissinger. The experience of visiting Russia and serving my country for this important meeting was overwhelming. It also presented me with new, valued credentials I believed would enhance my career.

By this time, I had almost 15 years of government service and had been in a management position for more than four years. Armed with a college degree and impressive credentials, I felt qualified to actively seek out career advancement. Human resource development is an essential part of the mission assigned to every personnel department in the federal government. The validity of this mission is obvious: the public is well served if the qualifications of every government employee are put to their highest and best use. As public servants improve their skills and knowledge, more responsibilities should be placed on them in order for the government to benefit.

Accordingly, I began frequent visits to State's personnel office, seeking help in changing career fields from communications supervision to an administrative position within the department. My belief was that such a move would benefit the department through expanded human resource utilization and benefit me by increasing my career opportunities. I had gone about as far as I was likely to go in a small unit such as the communications center and truly felt I could do more good in an expanded environment.

It soon became clear to me that, in the opinion of the personnel office, I was more of an annoyance than an asset to be better used. For generations, white males had gained entrance and advancement in administration at State by word-of-mouth through the "old boy" network. Your college roommate at your Ivy League school was more important for progression than mere qualifications. The ancient saying of "It's not what you know, but who you know" had prevailed so long that one expected to find it engraved in marble. However, in 1975, the department had finally been forced to establish a merit promotion system. Vacancies were supposed to be posted for public review and applications were to be actively considered. I was still naïve enough to believe that the new system would be honestly implemented. Given my employment experience, consistently outstanding appraisal ratings and new academic credentials, I was sure I would be selected immediately for the next vacancy.

My first five applications did not even result in an interview with a selecting official. Inquiring with personnel officials brought only the response that, while I was technically qualified, my credentials were not quite high enough to warrant an interview. Today, feminists speak loudly of a male-installed glass ceiling that keeps them down. But 25 years ago, I felt a steel wall erected to keep the black man out of the white man's club.

What they were telling me was nonsense. Many of the positions for which I applied were well below the level of GS-10, which I had held for some years. They would have been smarter to tell me I was overqualified than to assert that I didn't even rate an interview.

I visited with the director of personnel to discuss the fact that, no matter how many applications I submitted, his personnel specialists were not referring me to selecting officials for interviews. I pointed out that the merit promotion system was brand new and that guidelines for interview referral to selecting officials may require his attention. Surely, I pointed out, someone with my qualifications could not reasonably be denied interviews for positions carrying the same or lower grade level. The director's attitude was one of disinterest. He did not want to discuss his own departmental guidelines and didn't want to explore possibilities with me. I tried to get him to consider a lateral transfer to another office in order for me to gain the additional experience I seemed to need for advancement. His only response was to refer me to his personnel specialists even though he knew I had already met with them before coming to see him.

This was a much more difficult situation than being passed over for that promotion I had so surely earned. Without providing any reasons or offering a trace of assistance, the people in charge of human resource development were silently assuring themselves that, in spite of new regulations requiring merit promotions, things were going to go along as they always had at State.

At this time I sought out a young black man, John Gravely, who was doing very well at State. In fact, he was a rising star in the department and seemed to be entirely comfortable in black, white or mixed groups of professional employees. As I got to know him better, I could see that he was quite talented and wise beyond his years. We discussed my situation, frustration and growing anger on many occasions and he became a calming influence on me as I tried to work through the problem. He really became interested in me when I mentioned to him that his alma mater, American University, had accepted me into its graduate school. I took his advice concerning which graduate courses to take in order to better qualify for positions I hoped to achieve.

John soon transferred to the U.S. Department of Transportation, but we never lost touch and have remained friends to this day.

While I did not cease applying for positions that were at or below my qualification level, I concentrated on improvement through higher education and was accepted for graduate study at American University. Just getting into the school was an achievement since it has a national reputation for academic rigor. It was also a predominately white school, but so was Perth Amboy High and I had not felt any restraints imposed on me there.

To earn a graduate degree, one must maintain a minimum grade average of B. I knew this going in and believed that my ethic of hard work would see me through as it had done in my undergraduate studies. The first grade I received at American University was a C. I was devastated. In discussing the results with my classmates in the course, I learned that the professor had allowed two students to do extra course work in lieu of taking the final examination. No one I talked to had been offered the same opportunity. Since I felt confident that my work was at or above the B level, I asked the professor for reconsideration of the grade or the alternative, to let me have extra work assignments. He refused to consider either option.

This was another case of basic unfairness and there was still too much of my parents' upbringing in me to let it pass. I went to the dean of students and explained the situation. He agreed with my view that if any students were allowed extra work for grade improvement, all should be given the same opportunity. Shortly afterward the professor gave me an extra assignment which, when completed, resulted in a final grade of B for the course. Thus, I was allowed to continue in the graduate program. Some of my fellow black students were convinced that the professors were trying to flunk us out and pointed out that the two students initially permitted to do the extra work were white. It was impossible for me to agree or not agree. The only driving force in my actions had been striving for fair treatment.

There was a course in my field of study which had a reputation of resulting in top grades for those who did the work. I took it hoping to improve my grade point average. Basically, it involved an urban economic case study in which I developed a shopping location built on considerations of planning issues, marketing, land use and financial structure. I did not miss a day of class and performed extra research in order to perfect my case. When I submitted my work product I was confident that I had aced the course.

When the grades were posted, I had received a B. I noticed that the grades of several students who had skipped class frequently and appeared to me to have no interest in the work had received A's and B's. Having seen some of their limited work products, I couldn't believe the grades awarded. I approached both course professors and asked for reconsideration of my grade based on the quality of the case I had built. Initially, they refused. But a few days later, one of them called me and said that, after reconsideration, they had decided to raise my grade to an A.

Even in graduate school, it was obvious that I had to work twice as hard and actively oppose unequal treatment to stay even.

In 1977, I was awarded a master's degree in public administration from American University. State had paid the tuition for parts of the coursework which were directly related to professional fields in the department. Surely now, I believed, they could not continue denying me advancement or transfer based upon a lack of administrative credentials.

At this time, what I thought of as an encouraging event took place. A black man I had known in the department years earlier when he had worked in the passport office was appointed deputy assistant secretary for equal employment opportunity. Percy was a big man and liked to let folks know that he had played football for the University of Iowa in the 1959 Rose Bowl game. When I socialized with him during my first years in the department he had been very friendly, but we lost touch when he transferred to the Navy Department. Now he was back at State and in a high position.

After letting him settle into his new job for a month, I asked for a meeting with him, and he arranged it immediately. We had a thorough discussion of my history and situation in the department. Percy was supremely confident in his ability to help me and assumed an attitude that it would "be a piece of cake" to take care of my problems. I was somewhat shocked at his optimism because I doubted it would be an easy situation to resolve, but I was also genuinely relieved to finally have someone with authority in my corner.

Months went by, and I had no word from Percy. I finally called him to see how he was doing on my behalf. He told me about meetings he had held with various personnel officials and made vague references to having brought the matter up in discussions with the director general. In the end, all I got out of our conversation was the old bureaucratic axiom: "These things take time."

Later on, Percy called to tell me he had set up a meeting that day with an important personnel official who would resolve my situation. He said he would call me after the meeting and let me know the results. I waited hopefully for the rest of the day with my hand never far from the telephone, but Percy never called. That night, I attended a social event at the home of a fellow employee and ran into Percy. When I asked him how the meeting had gone, he dismissed me with, "Man I don't want to talk about equal employment opportunity tonight. I want to party!" I knew at that moment that his empty rhetoric placed him in the same category with all the other department officials from whom I had sought assistance over the years. His indifference was devastating because I knew and trusted him. I had emotionally relied on his offer of resolution and he had let me down. He stayed with the department for a few more years, then accepted an overseas position. He never contacted me again.

Nothing had changed with the good old boys at State. I spent the next five years constantly applying for vacant positions and being ignored, rebuffed and lied to by those charged with human resource development. The fight was on.

Going above the personnel director, I wrote a series of letters to the highest personnel authority in the department, the director general. My correspondence pointed out that I was bewildered by the department's refusal to let me change fields from a supervisory role to that of administration. I emphasized that the department had partially sponsored my graduate studies in public administration and, by this action alone, had encouraged my advancement in this direction. Why, I asked, encourage off-duty advanced education by employees if the department had no interest in utilizing the results? These and other questions posed by me to the director general and to many other high officials in the department went unanswered.

At one point, the director general delegated two officials from his office to discuss the matter with me. At least a response confirmed that I existed. The two officials, both black, met with me twice. At the end of the second meeting, they stated that within two months I would be reassigned to an administrative post within the department. By this time, I was only cautiously optimistic.

After three months of silence, I called each of the officials to inquire as to their progress on my transfer. One of them could not recall having suggested that I would be transferred to administration. The other simply encouraged me to keep applying for appropriate vacancies. She also added that I should consider applying for positions available in other federal agencies. Both of them were obviously covering up their promise to me and wanted to distance themselves from this matter.

I contacted a close friend, Clifton Smith, about my situation. Clifton was special assistant to the congressional delegate from the District of Columbia. We discussed several options and concluded that a different approach must be taken.

Deciding to elevate the fight, I not only wrote to my D.C. delegate, but I also wrote to the senator from my home state of New Jersey seeking their help in redressing the problem. Both of them wrote to the department seeking answers as to why a highly qualified, well-credentialed and experienced employee with numerous departmental commendations had not been able to advance or change career fields. The department's responses to these congressional inquiries not only failed to answer any of the questions, but also contained only rigid recitations of procedures, took no responsibility for any aspect of the subject and offered no hint of any possible resolution. I couldn't have been more disappointed. An objective reading of the letters simply conveyed the message that Eric Hughes was not worth dealing with. He should just go away.

In my heart, I knew that the department officials wanted their lives to continue as they had during the days before equal opportunity became the law. They were willing to put some blacks in visible positions as a genuflection in the direction of principle, but they had no intention of allowing genuinely pervasive competition on their own turf. Perhaps in the past they could wear down assertive blacks and make them roll over and play dead in the face of their invisible barriers, but this was a new day. If they made any mistake, it was in misjudging my character.

The fight was not over. I continued to apply for every appropriate vacancy posted under the merit promotion system. In many cases, I applied for positions well below my level and kept careful records of every result. Between 1975 and 1979, I applied for 49 job vacancies within State. I was granted an interview only twice and was never selected.

Only one case needs to be cited here to document what I was up against. I applied for a posted position of personnel management specialist, grade GS-7. Though it was three grades below my level, it would have allowed me to enter the personnel field. This was one of the areas of administration in which I felt I could excel given my years of experience as a managing supervisor. This was one of the two vacancies for which I was granted an interview. During the interview, the selecting official told me that while I had impressive credentials, I had no personnel experience. He later selected a white female secretary to be promoted to the post.

Meanwhile, a new director of communications had been appointed. As he grew into the job, he recognized that I had skills and potential beyond my current position. He asked me to undertake a special project to develop a comprehensive training manual for communications center employees which would include all the specific knowledge requirements, as well as sections on skills and attitude. He gave me no time limitations. I was both thrilled and thankful: it would give me a chance to create tangible proof of administrative skills and it verified that the new director was aware of my frustrations and wanted to help me break into new fields.

It is nearly impossible to explain what that detail did for my motivation and spirits. It took my mind off the daily feelings of frustration and rejection and the work itself renewed my confidence in my ability to perform complex administrative tasks. During the preparation, I had to meet with many other managers to include their ideas and to get their acceptance of my own. This activity was a confidence builder. At the end of one year, I completed the manual and it was accepted as policy without revision by upper management. The new director gave me an outstanding performance appraisal and a letter of commendation in which he acknowledged sustained exceptional achievement in the performance of official duties. I felt that nothing could have been more helpful for adding evidence of administrative and personnel experience to my credentials.

Coming off of this high, I then experienced the event which would be my final effort to achieve my goals within the daily operating routine of State. In the preceding four years, I had become friends with a high official of the department, a white male I'll call Derrick. We had breakfast together once a week and our conversations ranged from sports and politics to every aspect of work. We shared interests, including trends in men's fashions. It was purely a social relationship and being fully aware of my aspirations, Derrick often offered unofficial help. Even though he indicated he would be glad to talk with people on my behalf, I never took him up on it. I still thought I could do it on my own. While he and I often had breakfast together, he always spent his luncheons in the cafeteria surrounded by women employees, many of whom worked for him.

I applied for two posted personnel vacancies and later found that Derrick was the selecting official. I thought my day had finally come. But Derrick selected two white women who were members of his luncheon entourage. As soon as I could, I confronted him and asked him for an explanation. He said that he thought highly of me and would have welcomed me into his office but that I did not have the necessary experience. He said he would be too busy to find the time to train me in the skills I would need. I knew that the people he selected had some personnel experience at the lowest technical level, but none in personnel management. I also knew that neither held a college degree, nor any sort of administrative experience involving responsibility. Derrick knew from my file and from our friendship that I had taken many graduate courses in personnel management and had worked eight years directly supervising a staff which involved me in personnel work on a daily basis.

Thus ended any hope of finding equal employment opportunity at State. I had given at least five years of my life trying to vault the racial barricades built into the system and the only result had been a conspiracy of silence intoning the unspoken word that Eric Hughes was a troublemaker who should be rejected at every turn. What I thought had been a fight for justice and fair treatment had been only the opening skirmish. The time for war had come.

I contacted a close friend, Robert Clark, who had been a hearing examiner in EEOC. He sat down with me to draft a formal complaint. During this process, it was necessary for me to do some extensive research. One of the compelling findings I made was that the same director of personnel, who denied me every time I sought reassignment within the department, authorized during that same time period the reassignment of two white males. These reassignments had been made on a noncompetitive basis so that they were not advertised on the bulletin board and no one else could apply. In addition, the two reassignments were to positions with a career ladder potential of GS-14/15 and among the highest paid federal positions. Thus the same personnel director who constantly denied my reassignment had placed himself squarely in the midst of my discrimination complaint.

On June 20, 1979, I filed a formal discrimination complaint

against the department based on race and sex. Although the complaint was based on the two noncompetitive white male reassignments, my filing contained substantial evidence that the pattern of discrimination had been in continuous practice for at least six years. Finally, I did my best to document that the pattern of discrimination involved a general conspiracy since that was the only way 49 consecutive applications to fill vacancies could have received identical treatment by so many personnel officers.

A counselor was duly assigned to look into the complaint in an attempt to bring about an informal resolution. He interviewed several of the officials who had responsibility for my career development and with whom I had dealings over the years in question. They had their stories fairly well synchronized. All of them said they had done everything possible to assist me and vowed strong allegiance to every word in the letter and spirit of the merit promotion system. The person who had non-competitively reassigned the two white males claimed I wanted an unwarranted promotion. Apparently his selective memory overlooked all of my applications for vacancies far below my current grade of GS-10 and my requests for lateral reassignments. Not one of them offered any proposed resolution to the complaint.

The first formal investigation of my complaint was a whitewash (pun intended) from the outset. The white investigator never evidenced much interest in unearthing the truth and saw no conflict of interest problem in the fact that one of the people he had to interview was his own boss, who had denied one of my applications. His report concluded that I had not been a victim of discrimination and it recommended dismissal of the complaint.

The report was so incomplete and poorly done that I immediately demanded a reinvestigation by a disinterested, competent case officer. The report failed to present information about my allegations, contained no affidavits from key people familiar with my citations and contained no information concerning my applications for reassignment. The most egregious omission was the lack of any reference to the reassignment of two white males at the same time the responsible personnel officer was considering my application for reassignment.

After reviewing my long memorandum to the complaints section in which I outlined every discrepancy and omission in the investigative report, it was decreed that a supplemental investigation must be done. At the same time, the department announced it had more discrimination complaints to investigate than it had investigators. This backlogged condition would delay the reinvestigation of my case.

Delay can be a defensive tactic or it can be an unintended event. But in either case, it tends to weaken a complainant's position because memories fade and people get transferred to far away places. From December 1979 to September 1981, when the department finally hired a contract investigator to pursue my case, I wrote several letters to the complaints section urging timely reinvestigation and pointing out that the people listed in my complaint should be swiftly contacted and interrogated. Without my persistent attempts to move things along, my case probably would have languished even longer than the nearly two years it took the department to take it up again. I knew that final resolution could take years, but everything would rest on the investigation record and that needed to be handled in a timely manner.

During the entire period of my struggles within State, I had sent out several applications to other Washington-based agencies within the federal government. A flower burst forth from these seeds in January 1980 when I received a letter from the U.S. Department of Commerce notifying me that I had been selected for an intern program in its National Oceanic and Atmospheric Administration. I had applied with full knowledge that a downgrade would be required to enter the program. But I was joyful to accept that step down as the price of admission to an agency where numerous career advancement opportunities existed. I felt that the move could be the good break of my professional career and I intended to take every possible advantage of it. I was also happy to be away from State while my case was being processed.

In the early spring of 1980, my mother was hospitalized in Perth Amboy. She had been ill for some years and had never truly recovered from major surgery a few years earlier. I drove up to visit her and, after a couple of hours at her bedside, I called the nurse because Mom started to cough and was becoming nauseous. After the nurse left, I returned to her bedside and could see that she was very tired. I told her that I was going to leave for a while so that she could rest. When I got to the elevator, I turned around and went back to give Mom a hug and kiss. She passed on shortly afterward. Helen Hughes was a quintessential mother and grandmother and is missed by everyone who knew her.

In September 1981, a contract investigator was finally assigned

47

to my case, and he carried out a much more professional inquiry concerning the facts I cited in the formal complaint. His report set out as facts many of the allegations I had asserted. For instance, the file included official personnel records of the two white employees who had been reassigned to career advancing positions during the time I was fruitlessly seeking reassignment. The record this time clearly documented the signature of the personnel director who had denied me while approving the others without public notice. There was also documentation that the personnel director's claim that I wanted an unwarranted promotion was entirely false. Further, although the same personnel director had said my academic credentials were not directly related to the kind of work the department engaged in, the record now confirmed that I had taken graduate courses such as Manpower Utilization; Leadership for Public Management; Intergovernmental Fiscal Policy; Organization and Management Theory; Research for Management; The Administrative State; and Institute on Organizational Development and Change. Quite obviously, such subjects are directly related to the work of any government organization.

I wrote some remaining questions, comments, clarifications and rebuttals to the investigating office. The seemingly most important part of the case and investigative report had to do with the two white men being non-competitively reassigned. The department claimed that this happened through a "management development pool" program. I had never heard of this program and I certainly had never been given an opportunity to participate. In my written response, I asked questions concerning the "management development pool" and wanted to know who had been eligible to enter it and how many minorities were trained through it. These questions were not acknowledged.

In June 1982, a contract adjudicator reviewed the entire case and concluded that I had been subjected to disparate treatment in being denied reassignment in the manner of the two white men and that the only material distinction explaining the disparity was race. She also concluded that the continuous denial to me of reassignment also precluded my chances of getting the very experience I allegedly lacked in competing for the vacancies. Her recommendation was that I be promoted to the grade that the two white men had achieved. Victory on racial discrimination and victory on remedy had good tastes.

But of course, I felt good much too soon. In July 1982, the

department informed me that a proposed disposition had been reached, but additional information had been requested by a legal advisor before it could be cleared. Nothing was said about why or what additional information was being sought. Knowing the people at State, I sniffed the odor of a large, long-tailed rodent, but could do nothing.

In April 1983, State ordered a third investigation because of the lack of information in the original file explaining the personnel actions taken to reassign two white men similarly situated as myself. This "investigation" dissolved into variations of only two statements. A personnel official said that the two white men and I were not similarly situated because they were both outstanding employees at the GS-15 level while I was only a GS-11. I replied that my records reflected continuous outstanding appraisals and that if I had been given an equal opportunity for reassignment, I, too, could have been elevated to the GS-15 level.

At the beginning of the fifth year since the filing of my complaint, I still had no notice of a proposed disposition. I wrote and asked again when I could expect it and was told that a proposed settlement of my case was being drafted and would be presented in May 1984. That date came and went, so I wrote the congressional delegate from Washington and my home state senator from New Jersey again, enclosing a long chronology of the case. They both wrote State and asked when a settlement could be expected. The response they got from State was that it was awaiting information from me before it could develop a settlement agreement.

It turned out that State was considering offering me a position in the department and needed me to tell them the conditions under which I would return. I wasn't sure I wanted to return. There had been several cases there where an employee had won a discrimination case and been assigned to a position in which he could only fail. This kind of set-up was a well-known response in the department. After much thought, I informed them that I wanted a GS-15 grade, back pay, training and a position not subject to downgrading or reduction-in-force. The job had to be in Washington and there must be no retaliation for my filing the complaint.

In July 1985, State rejected any settlement conditions, issued final findings of no discrimination and proposed to dismiss my complaint. They rejected my allegations by saying that I did not meet the specialized work experience qualifications for the positions and by saying that I was not "similarly situated" in compari-

49

son with the two reassigned white men because we worked in different offices and therefore the managers who reassigned them had no responsibility to reassign me. Finally, they added a new point by saying that my complaint about the reassignment issue was not filed within the required 30-day filing period.

The first two of these statements could be easily rebutted and the third (the new issue of the 30-day limit) was a lie. They knew full well that I couldn't have known about it because it was done in secret and when I finally discovered it, I filed within 30 days. The problem was that the time for administrative relief had passed. With the same issuance of findings, the submission of rebuttals and refutations could only take place by adjudication.

It was put up or shut up time and I knew in my heart that I could not let them win by simply denying the truth. There had to be justice.

To hire an attorney and still fulfill my family obligations, I had to take a part-time job at a department store during nights and weekends, while still trying to excel in my full-time position at Commerce. It was a strain on everybody, but I had to do it or fail to defend myself. I worked mainly in the men's department for minimum wage. At times I had to do menial jobs, such as dusting clothes fixtures, sweeping floors and carrying filthy boxes. I also had to endure verbal abuse from group managers with deadlines to meet. After working all day at my professional job, I had to stand on my feet for another four hours every night and for ten or 12 hours on weekends when I could get the work.

The real cost of working nights and weekends to support my legal representation was a diminished family life. Dinner with my wife and two young daughters was impossible. Family outings were cancelled and I missed most of my daughters' school activities. Fortunately, Norma supported me completely and helped me deal with my guilt concerning not being with her and the children. Norma helped fill the void by taking the girls shopping and visiting family members and friends.

Since I had maintained good records over the years, it was not hard for my attorneys to grasp the essentials of my case. My recourse was to force a judicial hearing. Of course we hoped that State would settle prior to such a hearing once all our facts and allegations were on the table. But we had to be prepared for the full battle. As an opening salvo, my attorneys sent two comprehensive letters to State advising that a settlement would be in their best interest rather than risk the cost of a jury award.

They pointed out that the adjudicator's finding of discrimination against me had not been rejected in their final findings and the new timeliness of filing issues they had raised could be easily overcome and, in any case, had no effect on the core allegations.

As expected, State rejected our suggestion of settlement discussions. But they did propose another step prior to litigation. They recommended a review and hearing by EEOC, a government agency separate from the department. This was another major letdown for me since I had entertained real hopes that our letters were compelling enough to get us into settlement proceedings. However, my confidence in the righteousness of our cause was not diminished and we agreed to go forward.

The hearing was scheduled for May 20, 1986. During a pre-hearing conference, the EEOC attorney outlined all the procedures and, interestingly, urged settlement of the matter before the hearing.

My attorney asked me to calculate how much I would receive in backpay if a settlement was reached that included such compensation. This was a difficult task since the case went back as far as 1974. I had to locate copies of old federal pay scales for those years. I didn't mind doing the research, but I felt the calculations should have been the lawyer's job since he would have to defend them in negotiation if it ever got that far.

I began to become uncomfortable with my representation. When I called my attorney it was often days before he returned my call. Frequently on office visits, I would have to wait more than an hour beyond the appointed time to see him. Just as I began to seriously consider changing counsel to someone who would understand the importance of my prevailing in this matter, I received a letter from him saying he had to have an operation and would need to postpone the hearing for three months.

Emotionally, I could not tolerate another substantial delay. Obviously sickness wasn't the fault of anyone, but I didn't believe I could wait. A good friend recommended a top attorney who had, in fact, won several cases against State. I called her immediately and setup an initial consultation.

June Kalijarvi had to be one of the most physically diminutive, white lawyers among all of the many thousands of attorneys who housed themselves along Washington's "K Street Canyon." Not only was she a tiny woman, but her well-dressed appearance and informal demeanor gave the impression of someone less than formidable. After a long conference, my impression changed completely. Obviously she had much experience in employment discrimination and had an aggressive style that, I would soon learn, couldn't be intimidated. By the end of our meeting, she had gained my respect and I was pleased that she agreed to take over my representation. We sent our change of counsel notifications to all parties and the hearing was reset for the following month. Ms. Kalijarvi reopened settlement negotiations while we waited for the hearing.

Just before the hearing date, June called me with the news that State had made a substantial cash offer to settle the case. At first, I didn't know what to say. My head swirled with thoughts about how I struggled to pay my attorneys fees; the sacrifices thrust upon my family to support me in my insistence on justice; and the very bumpy road traveled to reach it. Even though we had talked about settlement many times, it is quite different when you actually face it. While State would get away without admitting to discrimination, the world would know I won because the government never would have agreed to such a large settlement otherwise. It took only several minutes for me to agree. The sense of relief that I could finally get on with life and the reality of vindication were enormous. On June 12, 1986 I signed the settlement agreement. My only regret was that the document forbade me to divulge the monetary amount or other terms of the agreement. I would have shouted them from the rooftops.

When the news broke at State, my telephone rang almost constantly. Every black employee wanted to congratulate me; most wanted to thank me for battling one of the most discriminatory departments in government. Many said they had known Goliath was white but now they knew David was black; and others, who had pending cases, told me how I had inspired them to persevere. A lot of the calls were from total strangers who simply wanted me to know how important my victory was to them.

I remember wishing that my parents could have lived to witness this victory since much of it was due to them. They gave me strength of character by including me in their lifelong struggle against unfairness in all its ugly forms. They were part of this. Their hard work, faith in God and refusal to ever give up had always been a quiet inspiration to me. In a real sense, they had won, too.

As the days passed and the reality sank in, I thought a lot

about what our black leaders were saying to whites. Little snippets from the biography of Malcolm X, the black Muslim leader, came back to me: "The American black man is the world's most shameful case of minority oppression" and "Four hundred years of black blood and sweat are invested here in America and the white man still has the black man begging for what every white immigrant fresh off the ship can take for granted the minute he walks down the gangplank."

I also recalled some of what Clifford Alexander, the first African-American Secretary of the Army, said to a senate committee a few years earlier. "You (white Americans) see us as less than you are. You think that we are not as smart, not as energetic, not as well suited to supervise; that we are looking for something extra – a government program that gives us something we do not deserve. You think that our sons and daughters are taking places in colleges that if the world were only 'fair' would go to your white children instead. White men and women can develop the solutions…(while) black men can only nibble at the edges of power in America. During my lifetime no black person will join your exclusive senate club, run a *Fortune 500* company, be president of NBC, CBS, CNN or ABC. No black will become president of an Ivy League school or be head of the Kennedy Center. You are determined to reserve those powerful positions for your own kind. Yes, we nibble at the edges while you enjoy hearty meals."

I believe that Mr. Alexander summed up the American racial situation beautifully. Racism is real and everywhere. He said that blacks continue to be left on the outside of success, with the exception of a very few such as Colin Powell, Oprah Winfrey and Michael Jordan. With the removal of the racism cloak, however, there could be many, many more.

Winning the case made me think through and face scars that had lingered within me for a long time. I am truly distrustful of the white system. It was not created with inclusiveness as a goal. Even though I grew up in a mostly white community, I realized that most of them would not respect blacks regardless of the person's qualifications or experience. It's true that many whites will go out of their way to diminish the integrity and contributions of black employees. Yes, I am bitter. I also know that bitterness left unchecked can become all consuming and, at that point, the black man is of no further use to anyone. How to face life in a frequently hostile white world? The only code I can set for myself and hopefully for those who follow me, is to lead as decent a life as possible but to never countenance bigotry—ever.

News of my settlement got a brief article in *Jet* magazine in the July 7, 1986 issue and caused me to receive congratulations from African-Americans around the country.

In those days and even today, the Engine Room of the Pier Seven restaurant on the southwest Washington waterfront was a watering hole for black professionals. A few days after my settlement announcement, I was there after work with some friends when Percy joined us. I hadn't seen him in seven years. He attempted to congratulate me, but I refused his handshake. For just a moment, I saw in his eyes recognition of his unkept promises to me and I hoped he saw the bitterness in mine.

During the arduous years of my struggle with State, I told everyone that, if I prevailed, I would have a memorable victory party. Many times, it had seemed a far away dream. But now was the time to put that dream into action. I had a long list of supporters to invite and I especially wanted to include as many black employees from State as possible because so many of them were being denied their rights everyday.

On Nov. 14, 1986, I threw a party for 375 people that is remembered and spoken of to this day. I wanted everybody to share my joy and to also see me when I wasn't suffering. The congressional delegate from the District of Columbia was the keynote speaker and had many complimentary words to say about my crusade and resulting victory. He said, "History is nourished by the instructive example of Eric's 12-year struggle for justice at State and Eric's victory has vindicated Martin Luther King, Jr.'s struggle to end racial and employment discrimination. Eric's victory will be a source of inspiration to the black (congressional) caucus who continue to prevent those who would turn back affirmative action and equal employment opportunity." Congressman Walter Fauntroy ended by reciting an old Irish blessing:

> May the road rise to meet you,
> May the wind be always at your back,
> May the sun shine upon your face,
> And may the rains fall softly upon your fields.
> And until we meet again,
> May God hold you in the palm of his hand.

I've thought about that speech many times and I truly believe that it got me through the struggles for justice that I did not know then were coming my way.

Eric and Norma's wedding day

Celebration for Receiving Masters Degree

Eric Hughes and fellow graduate Frank Deflorimonte

Mr. & Mrs. Eric Hughes

YALTA – USSR 1974

No.OR–10

ERIC HUGHES

Visit of President Nixon

Eric Hughes' name tag for Presidential trip to Yalta, Russia

left to right — Clifton Smith, former D.C. Delegate Walter E. Fauntroy, Eric Hughes and Attorney June Kalijarvi

left to right — Eric Hughes, Walter E. Fauntroy, Malachi Knowles and June Kalijarvi

left to right — Clifton Smith, Walter E. Fauntroy, Eric Hughes,
June Kalijarvi and Malachi Knowles

Family — left to right
Betty Hughes, Cynthia Moore, Beateal Gumbs, Tracy Holbert,
Aaron Hughes, Norma Hughes, Wendy Hughes, Calvin Hughes,
Ruth Hughes, Winston Hughes and Eric Hughes

left to right — Eric Hughes, Aaron Hughes, Calvin Hughes and
Winston Hughes

left to right — Clifton Smith, Norma Hughes and Eric Hughes

left to right — Arvell Greenwood, Clifton Smith and Eric Hughes

Party participants

CHAPTER FIVE

The National Oceanic and Atmospheric Administration was a relatively new agency set up within the existing U.S. Department of Commerce. It had been put together by taking a number of traditional units from within Commerce, such as the Weather Bureau and the National Coastal and Geodetic Survey, together with units from agencies outside of Commerce and piling them together in an effort to create a single unit of government responsible for studying, monitoring, reporting, regulating and, in some cases, protecting and nurturing certain areas of our environment. In the process of creating it, Congress, in its traditional wisdom, added some new creations and gave up on consolidation in many important areas. For instance, Congress could not wrest the Coast Guard from the bureaucratic clutches of the Treasury Department, even though it made sense for the agency newly responsible for our coasts to have some boats with which to do its job.

By 1980, the new agency was still in something of a shakedown mode in trying to organize itself and integrate the many offices that had been thrown in to create it. In a gesture toward consistency among the disparate units within the agency, the Office of Equal Employment Opportunity set up a task force to review all job series, with an eye toward sorting out the numbers and relative percentages of minorities and women serving in the various operating units, and then they were to take remedial action in offices with too few minorities in professional positions. NOAA created the Post Graduate Intern Program, which was a vehicle to recruit professional minorities and women from throughout the federal government and insert them into organizational units requiring racial or gender balance.

I became a part of Commerce in 1980 when I was selected for the intern plan and assigned to the Office of Ocean and Coastal Resources Management. One might expect that an organization with such an important sounding name would be rather large and powerful. When, in fact, it was a group of about 80 people, predominately young white men and women, trying to assist coastal states to protect and manage their water's edge and estuarine resources. In addition to the offices of the director and general counsel, there were four operating units: Coastal Programs Division, Sanctuaries and Reserves Division, Ocean Minerals and Energy Division and a unit called the Policy and Coordination Division. The principal tool available to the office was a program offering grant funds to coastal states for projects and programs which promoted goals, such as environmental education, scientific research, marine sanctuaries and marine life protection.

My appointment was as a GS-9 program assistant in the Coastal Programs Division. This unit had about 30 people to handle five regions: South Atlantic, Gulf Coast, Great Lakes, North Atlantic and Pacific. Each region had a staff of three or four professionals, including a manager. I was one of three black professionals in the division. Another was a woman who I'll call Kim. All five of the secretaries were black.

On my first day at work, I received some curious stares and was asked the usual questions of a newcomer: where had I worked before, where had I gone to school, what degrees did I hold and so on. The questions themselves were innocuous enough, but the tone of voice and inflection had an edge which was more competitive than welcoming. I guess my defenses were up because my first impression was one of a group of mostly white people believing themselves to be part of an elite group and trying to figure out how a black professional came to be in their midst.

It didn't take many days for me to get the lay of the land. Many of the employees were just out of college and had no work experience. Several others had only a few years in federal service. Their backgrounds included advanced degrees in scientific areas, such as biology and geology, as well as more general fields, such as public administration. The nature of their work tended to give them a sense of power because each could strongly influence the granting or withholding of federal money and technical assistance to the states assigned to them. Many of the staff used this limited power to demonstrate how tough they could be on certain states by denying proposed projects or making applicants go through an arduous process to gain approval. It sometimes seemed that staff professionals were rewarded with promotions, high performance ratings, cash awards and choice travel assignments for nothing more noteworthy than presenting the appearance of toughness toward allegedly recalcitrant states.

Two early observations were potential portends for my future in the office. Professionals who had been in place long enough to influence the filling of vacancies recommended friends from their *alma maters*. At least six professionals were from one school and four from another. Even though the office itself was new and the vast majority of staff relatively young, the "old boy" network was already hard at work and growing. The other observation was more worrisome. My white boss, whom I'll call Bill, knew that I had no practical background in science, oceans, or grants management, but took no interest in helping me learn the things I needed to know in order to contribute. When I asked him about a training program, he made it clear that there was none and whatever learning was necessary had to be done on the job. He was a regional manager, but his answers to my questions were either evasive or evidence that he just didn't know the answers. As time went on, the most charitable opinion of him I could reach was that he was lazy, uninterested in his job and did the bare minimum to survive. To prosper in this environment, I would only have my own initiative and drive.

Putting aside these two clouds on my horizon, however, I could also see that the office itself, and the Coastal Programs Division within it, was replete with career opportunities. It was a young and growing outfit without the inviolable traditions that decades of service tends to create in organizations. The missions were worthy and the goals lofty. Frequent travel, often to desirable places such as the U.S. Virgin Islands, Puerto Rico and Hawaii, was necessary. Working with state officials and coordinating federal assistance grants and programs for them was infinitely more interesting and challenging than supervising the encoding and decoding of endless telegrams.

My enthusiasm led to determination. I was not going to be sidetracked by distractions. This was going to be my chance to grow and succeed.

The first thing I did was start taking night courses in subjects such as grants management, ocean environments and intergovernmental operations. I threw myself into the work, asked questions of everyone and, when Bill failed to give me assignments, I regularly studied coastal management regulations and reviewed regional state programs on my own. In less than a year, my internship ended and I was promoted to program officer with the grade of GS-11.

The position description of a program officer calls for assignment to a state so that a specific person is designated to interact with state officials and to coordinate federal grants and programs. Instead of assigning me to a state, Bill had me doing other chores. I thought perhaps his reluctance to make the assignment had to do with lack of specific training, so I continued to ask him for a training program. Probably because of my badgering, Bill finally held a series of four training sessions with me. It was both shocking and ineffective because all I learned was that Bill knew very little about the subject matter under discussion and had no suggestions to offer.

Phil, the director of the office who had hired me into the internship program, noticed that I was not providing information on the region and learned the reason was that I had no state assignment. He told Bill to assign me to a state and, with visible reluctance, Bill assigned me to South Carolina.

This relieved me of my growing concerns about not being permitted to fulfill my position duties. As soon as I began meeting and working with South Carolina's officials, I found that I truly enjoyed the experience. It was so refreshing to be working with good people in efforts to solve real problems, that I felt increasingly at ease as my confidence grew concerning my new career.

I did my best to ignore racial overtones when they arose. I knew that South Carolina had been one of the most strictly segregated states in the nation until federal civil rights laws enforced desegregation in almost every aspect of public life. These were recent changes and people were still getting used to them. Most state employees that worked on coastal issues were white and all the local special interest groups that followed our programs seemed to be completely white. Many were shocked to see a black federal official come to their state to discuss coastal matters. I was often the only black person in meetings of 20 or more. When I went to the state capital in Columbia to discuss issues with legislative staff members, I often felt their discomfort with having to actually listen to and interact with a black person. Sometimes a state program manager would telephone my supervisor to discuss matters in my area of responsibility only to be told to talk to me directly.

These reactions were to be expected from southern state officials and the racial aspects of my interaction with South Carolina officials did not sour my work or truly interfere with my ability to carry out the functions of our office.

It was much harder to rise above racial insults in our own Washington offices where they should never have been permitted.

Every office has someone who thinks of himself as a joker. In our case it was a white man I'll call Jack because he really belongs in a box somewhere. He was a Midwesterner whose sloppy attire was exceeded only by his beer belly. He was of average height, mustached, opinionated and, unfortunately, outspoken. His dislike of all minority groups was thinly veiled only when he was on his best behavior. He had started working in the office when it was first created and many of the youngest employees thought this made him the resident expert on all matters. Some even laughed at his jokes.

When Ronald Reagan won the 1980 election, many people were well aware that one of his campaign promises was to cut numerous programs benefiting minorities. Jack stood in the central hallway and shouted, "You blacks better watch out now, because you won't be getting a free ride anymore with Reagan in office." I went over to him, asked what his problem was and told him never to do that again. He said nothing and gave me a look that seemed to say, "What's wrong with you?" and simply walked away. Even some of the whites in the office seemed startled by his outburst. Jack, of course, was not the only one in the office with such opinions. He was just the loudest.

Staff meetings were convened every Monday morning by the director. He would always open it by talking about pending legislation that might affect our programs, what was happening on Capitol Hill of interest to us, national issues of importance and initiatives being taken by other federal agencies. Then, he would go around the table asking each of the five regions to report on events in their geographic areas. At this point, the meetings usually degenerated to an almost juvenile "show and tell" session during which people could brag about how much federal money had been saved by their toughness or outright denial of money to their states. Others bragged about how their states were doing so well in order to suggest it was because of their aggressive efforts. Each such story would only encourage the next speaker to top it. On those occasions when a black professional spoke about his or her region, I would watch the white employees do their best not to listen. Sometimes a black participant would work for days before a meeting in order to provide solid information on an issue, but I never detected a look of respect on anyone's face.

In October 1981, the office went through a complete reorganization and I was assigned to the Pacific Region. My new white supervisor, a 28-year-old regional manager named Richard, was smart, aggressive and interested in solid results. I gained an enormous amount of experience while working with him because he wanted every member of his staff to succeed and was willing to help them do it. I was supposed to work with two states in our region but was assigned four due to personnel shortages. Despite the heavy workload, I handled my assignments efficiently and on time. Richard gave me my first outstanding appraisal.

Less fortuitous changes began the following month. A new director, Robert, and deputy director, Tony, were appointed by the Reagan Administration to take over the Office of Ocean and Coastal Resources Management. Robert never made any attempt to manage the office. He left all decisions to Tony and concentrated on his real mission, which was to dismantle the office. In the end, he was unable to accomplish killing off the program because the states, many of which were Republican, wanted it badly enough to lobby strongly for its retention. They, and the special interest groups, including major environmental organizations, were able to rally enough political support in Congress and the Administration itself to prevent Robert from completing his important assignment.

Tony was a white, 30-year-old New Yorker with an attitude. To say that he was brash in addition to arrogant is charitable. Thoughtfulness and respect for others were not among his virtues. More than once he called a person an idiot in front of the staff and he did not believe in deleting expletives when dressing down others or commenting on issues facing the office. Before long he had organized an informal team (predominately white women) to carry out his whims and he rewarded them with frivolous business trips, awards and stellar performance appraisals. Tony's theory of management was to keep his managers in constant trepidation and his program constituents, the state program managers, continuously fearful of being cut off if they didn't properly fulfill his every wish. He made no secret about not liking black people, but we were not alone since there were a lot of other people he didn't like either.

Things got even worse when a person named Edward came in

as our new chief of the Coastal Programs Division. He was a red-haired white man, sloppy and overweight, who literally enjoyed using power to manipulate. Our division managed a grant program of about 40 million dollars to help states achieve well-stated federal objectives. Even though there was a set formula for dividing up funds among the recipients, Edward exercised considerable discretion as to how the funds were spent for special projects and in deciding which states were awarded surplus funds. He could, and did, use his staff to manipulate awarding funds according to his personal agenda rather than the priority of any state.

The professional managers, such as my boss, Richard, were zealots of neither Republican nor Democratic party politics. They were executives whose job it was to carry out laws and regulations. They had to serve under the new appointees, but the majority of them were privately disgusted with the favoritism and manipulation.

The few black staff members, none of us favorites with the new management, had an additional burden. The United States Territories (American Samoa, Northern Mariana Islands, Guam, Puerto Rico and the U.S. Virgin Islands) have populations consisting almost entirely of minority groups. Islands have compelling coastal problems. The majority of their residents exist well below any definition of the poverty line, so these islands lack the wealth to internally generate the taxes necessary for major public programs. Edward felt uncomfortable around us and he had an agenda which included, at best, only token support for the Territories. But it was not a sufficient set of reasons for us to join his efforts to treat them differently.

Edward thought he was clever and the fact that he was often caught in his lies to various staff caused him not the least embarrassment. During his tenure, he allowed favorite white staff members to do pretty much as they pleased, even if it was against policy, and he ignored staff members who had failed to make his private list of favorites. The only thing that made him move quickly was any opportunity to take full credit for something achieved by his or anyone else's staff.

He handled job interviews in such a way as to favor those he had already decided he wanted and even used tricks to get his friends placed in positions he didn't directly control. Edward also selected favored white women employees for placement in positions where he could influence their advancement and he considered blacks non-essential employees. While he would never know-ingly afford an opportunity to any black employee, he also had his list of white staffers that suffered the same fate.

The regular performance appraisal process constitutes the offi-cial record of employment achievement (or lack thereof) in the fed-eral workforce. It is the basis for promotions, demotions, awards, transfers and almost all other personnel actions. It is so important in the life of public servants that there are books written about administering them. A host of management training programs dwell at length on the rules to be followed when filling them out in appraising employee performance and there are appeal processes subordinates can follow if they believe they've been unfairly judged. Lives can be damaged and careers ended with inappropri-ate or erroneous grades entered on these forms. Edward regarded employee appraisals as weapons to reward allies or to oppose ene-mies.

Tony and Edward worked closely together. Their decisions were primarily political and they often approved a project for fed-eral funding by well-connected political allies and disregarded the fact that these recipients had terrible performance records, poor reporting procedures and no history of achieving any results. It did-n't take long for our office's name to get tarnished in Congress, the states, private interest groups and within Commerce itself.

Having no other choice, I simply kept a low profile and con-tinued to work as hard as I could for the Pacific Region. Because the Pacific territories have unique problems and are a long way from Washington, the workload was heavy and travel extensive. I became eligible for promotion to GS-12 in June 1982. When it did-n't happen, I brought up the matter with Tony and Edward. They had been able to block it by pointing to a policy of having no more than one GS-12 slot in each region and the Pacific Region already had a black woman at that level. This was, of course, false and I named a region that had two white GS-12 females working within it. They ignored this fact.

Richard could not act openly against them even though he agreed with me that the action was unfair. Instead, he gave me the opportunity over the coming months to perform some assignments which could result in a commendation. Here is part of the text he wrote after I had finished the tasks:

Eric Hughes' performance has been exemplary and deserves special recognition. In discharging responsibilities, he has displayed a high degree of professionalism and initiative. Eric was immediately faced with helping resolve some of the most difficult and outstanding problems associated with any of the eight states in this region. In less than two months, he gained a basic understanding of the program and was able to provide a written recommendation for determining whether or not the state met a grant condition related to state management of islands adjacent to the shoreline. His performance of this task is noteworthy because he had no previous knowledge of the program and little experience in dealing directly with programmatic issues of such complexity and visibility. He spent intensive hours of reading beyond normal work hours and discussing the program and his task with other staff and units of the office. Moreover, when called on to assume the duties of acting regional manager, he did so without hesitation and successfully. As a result of his willingness to take on added responsibilities, the Pacific regional manager was able to devote more of his time to other states and major changes now affecting the federal program. In short, in five months, Eric has accepted an enormous workload and with a high degree of individual initiative has performed beyond what was expected under the circumstances. As a result, he has continued to improve his professional skills and understanding of office regulations, policies and procedures to the extent that he is likely to be able to perform the duties associated with the next higher level. This record of performance is exemplary and deserves recognition. I recommend that Eric should be considered for a promotion if and when a position becomes available.

The immediate effect of Richard's write up was an increase in my salary. But it had been designed to get me promoted. Even Tony and Edward could not avoid the issue in the face of Richard's high praise; and, after stalling long enough to emphasize their power, I was promoted to GS-12 and assistant regional manager in May 1983.

I would never diminish my respect or gratitude for Richard's support, but I also couldn't help resenting the fact that white employees in other regions were doing substantially less work and getting promotions routinely. Of course, some of them were getting promotions for no better reasons than Tony and Edward's blatant favoritism. But I still had to conclude that a black man needed two years of extraordinary effort to achieve what was routine in one year for whites in the office.

Sometimes racial insensitivity was evidenced in public outside the office. I was once attending a meeting in Seattle with 15 local and state government personnel. I was the program specialist and was accompanied by Bud, an evaluator from our office in Washington. As usual I was the only black person at the meeting. Normally, it rains most days in Seattle. But this was one of those rare, beautiful, sunny days. Like Jack, whom I've already described, Bud thought of himself as a joker and often said foolish things just to get accepted. Just as the meeting was opening, he said, "Eric doesn't have to worry about his skin color coming off because it's not raining today." I almost did not resist the temptation to rise up and hit him. After the meeting, several people told me how sorry they were and expressed their shock at such a tasteless and unfortunate a comment. More than one mentioned surprise that I was able to go on with the meeting. I certainly hadn't wished to continue with the meeting. But if a black man walked out of every situation where a gratuitous insult was passed, he might as well stay home.

I continued to expend my best efforts dealing with the heavy workload. In 1984, I received an award for successfully managing twice the amount of a normal workload. Richard's write up for the award said:

> Normally, Mr. Hughes would have managed the provision of staff services in two of the states in the region. During the past year, the region was confronted with a shortage of staff. Mr. Hughes willingly accepted responsibility for managing the additional workload. He provided staff services to four states and successfully completed the associated work. He did so in an independent, timely and

dependable way. In addition, he provided full support to the management of an unusually complicated and controversial amendment to a state coastal zone program in the region. His exemplary performance in successfully managing this unusually heavy and difficult workload enabled the region to continue to provide the basic programmatic services to the states in the region that otherwise would not have been possible. This resulted in estimated tangible savings to the government of one-third of a person's yearly salary at the GS-12 level, or approximately $10,000 in improved productivity.

In June 1984, the Pacific Region was finally assigned additional staff to assist with our work overload. Two white women, Mary and Betty, became our co-workers. Richard worked closely with them to help them absorb all they would need to know to help us. I was also involved in some of their training when Richard was absent from the office. For the next seven months, Richard assisted in bringing them up to speed in the region's procedures, but things were very busy and my duties were largely elsewhere. Consequently, I didn't get to know them well.

In April 1985, Richard accepted a position out of the area and resigned abruptly. I had seen his disgust with the manner in which Tony and Edward managed the office, so his resignation was not a total surprise to me. I was appointed acting regional manager. This probably happened because Edward and Tony had little choice. Richard's departure was so sudden, there had been no time for them to ease in one of their chosen people.

As a rule, blacks did not participate in office social affairs. Since we rarely felt welcome at work, there was no reason to expect it elsewhere. When I received an invitation to Richard's farewell party, however, I simply could not ignore it. He had been supportive of me in every way he could and I felt the need to express that by being there. As expected, I was the only black person present. Everyone was outwardly cordial, but I had no urge to linger.

Shortly after my appointment as acting regional manager, I held a staff meeting to discuss how I wanted our work handled and the relationships with our states that I hoped we could develop. It seemed to go well and I felt optimistic.

I was glad to have Mary and Betty on the staff. With Richard gone and my having to concentrate much more on office management than field work, the Pacific Region needed all the professionals we could get.

Mary had a master's degree in geology and had worked in state government on the west coast before joining the federal government. She seemed bright and aggressive. I had noticed that when she first arrived, several months before Richard's departure, she made it a point to introduce herself to everyone in the office and could be frequently seen in conversation with various staffers. What I had not realized was that she had been simply sniffing out the power structure and had managed to convince Edward and Tony that she was their rising star even before having accomplished her first work assignment. Now that I had taken over management of the region, it was necessary for me to be in almost daily contact with her. Unfortunately, it didn't go well from the beginning.

We've all had experiences where, upon first meeting someone, the encounter and conversation had been entirely proper and outwardly friendly, but afterward you had an almost definable sense of distrust or danger ahead. I don't think such subliminal impressions need be essentially race-based; they can just happen between humans. In the case of a black person, such an encounter with a white person – especially in a subordinate relationship, automatically carries the added weight of race questions. Does she dislike or disrespect me because I'm black, because I'm in charge, or both? Once someone has spent half a lifetime dealing with daily evidence that white people see us as less than they are, it becomes extraordinarily hard not to associate immediate disrespect with race. In my first encounter with Mary, I felt all of these things. Without being able to put my finger on a single thing she said, I came away with the impression that she was both cocky and dangerous. I had to do my best not to show any reciprocal feelings.

Soon enough, however, I had more than sufficient examples of her conduct to confirm these impressions. From the outset, she clung to Edward and Tony and either avoided or undercut me. She would discuss regional issues and her work assignments with Tony or Edward without coming to me first and, after attending meetings, would report the results to them without informing me of the meeting contents or decisions made during it.

In a normal leadership structure, such acts of insubordination are halted immediately by higher managers simply instructing the subordinate to operate through the immediate supervisor instead of reporting directly to them. If Edward and Tony had been professional leaders and competent enough to understand that senior executives must support managers below them, Mary's devious behavior would have been terminated after the first instance. However, this was the sort of office politics in which Edward an Tony reveled. They not only encouraged such informal alliances and ignored the principles of orderly management, they also thrived on them. In itself, a continuation of such subtle misconduct can be dismissed as immaturity or downright childishness. Left unchecked, it can spread and eventually destroy an organization.

Betty had a master's degree in marine affairs. She evidenced more seriousness about her work. She was bright and assertive, her style was both tactful and professional. I knew that neither she nor Mary had ever worked for a black supervisor before, so I wanted to go the extra mile to try establishing good working relationships.

I went to both Edward and Tony after each of the initial occurrences when Mary went around me. I asked them both to send her back to me when she brought up matters concerning the Pacific Region. They didn't afford me the courtesy of lip service and simply ignored my appeals. It wasn't long before I noticed Mary and Betty in frequent low-toned discussions with each other in the hallways. Soon after, Betty adopted Mary's pattern of excluding me and going directly to Edward or Tony with regional matters.

I held several meetings with Mary and Betty during which I urged them to follow office procedures and policies and stressed the importance of proper reporting relationships in the orderly accomplishment of regional goals. They were unresponsive and the situation soon got so bad that Mary decided she did not have to call me when she was late or advise me if she attended a meeting out of the office which would prevent her from reporting to work on time. As the problem became evident throughout the office, my continuing efforts to rein them into proper conduct and their on-going office socialization seemed to result in their looking like victims with Eric Hughes, the villain.

Every employee in the federal government has a right to request that upper-level management attend a performance appraisal meeting with his or her immediate supervisor. In Commerce, the categories available for a supervisor to record on the appraisal form are: outstanding, commendable, fully successful and unsatisfactory. When the time came for me to handle the performance appraisals for Mary and Betty, they exercised their rights and had both Edward

and Tony attend the appraisal meeting with me. I opened the meeting by recommending that both employees coordinate more fully with me in conducting their work and that they call the office when they knew they would be late or absent. Their response was to complain to Edward and Tony that such recommendations were unfair. Every point I covered in the meeting had the same response and in no case did I receive a hint of support from Edward or Tony.

When the time came for me to write up Mary and Betty's formal appraisals, I received instructions from Edward and Tony not to do so. They said they would handle it. This was entirely outside of department personnel policy. Performance appraisals had to be filled out by the first-line supervisor, then submitted to higher management who could, if they wished, record their own comments on the initial appraisal. Accordingly, I filled out the appraisals and submitted them. Tony and Edward had never felt it necessary to follow department policies which didn't suit their immediate purposes. So, they threw out my submission and wrote their own which awarded "outstanding" performance ratings to both women.

By this time, I could no longer deny admitting to myself the underlying strategy behind Edward and Tony's outrageous behavior. It was a setup. As acting regional manager, I had to be considered for promotion to permanent regional manager at some point. They could delay making the decision and had been doing so. But before long they would be required to act. Once they could offer proof that I was an ineffective manager, they could justify passing over me and bringing in another crony. It was only a matter of time before the other shoe would fall.

During this time, another person on my staff, a black woman named Lisa, came up for performance appraisal. Edward had been attempting to terminate her for some time and she had filed a discrimination complaint against him. My problem was that she actually was not performing up to standard levels and, as her supervisor, I had little choice in handling her rating. Without asking my opinion, Edward came to me and insisted that I give Lisa an unsatisfactory rating. I recorded her poor performance on the appraisal form because it was the truth, not because of Edward's interference in personnel procedures. Who would ever believe me?

The fact of being ignored in appraising whites and simultaneously being forced to appear as assisting in firing a black employee, along with the clear violations of set policies concerning personnel procedures, led me to write a strong memorandum of protest to Edward. It did absolutely no good, but at least it was on record.

Things continued in the same pattern. When I took a day of annual leave, Tony decided to send Mary to the state of Washington to represent the office on a boat cruise to discuss an organization's prospects of applying for federal funds. As acting regional manager for the Pacific Region, this was a conference I should have attended. When I asked Tony about it, he replied that he could not find me at the time the decision had to be made. On another occasion, Mary and I were attending a conference in Hawaii. Tony had been scheduled to give the opening remarks. At the last minute, he decided not to attend and appointed Mary, my subordinate, to replace him for that portion of the program. When I called Tony about it, he said, "I want to give her some exposure." At my insistence, I replaced Tony on the agenda. No one I could recall had ever wanted to give me "exposure."

When my term as acting regional manager was up, there was no competitive position vacancy posted and no applicants sought. Edward hired a white, political appointee named Bert and, thereby, ended my hopes of promotion.

It would have been easy to demonstrate resentment against Bert, but he had played no part in Edward's schemes. And, I knew that any overt action on my part would have only negative results at this point. Bert turned out to be a friendly, cordial and intelligent young man. During the time I worked with him, he was never less than fair in every action which, based on my experiences, is high praise indeed. I worked closely with him for the next several weeks to fill him in on the regional issues facing the office, staff duties and all the matters of importance coming under his direct management.

Shortly after Bert's appointment, my own appraisal period came up. Bert asked me to give him information on what I had done prior to his arrival since he had not been there to appraise it. I responded with the material he needed and Bert discussed it with Edward. My rating came back as "commendable." There may have been nothing I could do about being passed over for promotion, but to have an appraisal of less than "outstanding" was too unfair to let stand. I informed both Bert and Edward that the appraisal was unacceptable and, according to proper procedure, provided them with substantial documentary evidence to back up my assertion. The unspoken truth was that Edward and Tony could not be allowed to grant outstanding ratings to Mary and Betty while downgrading my performance. It only piled insult onto injury. My action in rejecting the appraisal was public notice that this time I intended to fight.

Edward, surprisingly, turned the matter over to Tony. I met with him and discussed only the merits of my case. Not a word was said between us about the real situation, but Tony could not have failed to understand I was very serious about my intention to take the matter as far as it would go. Later on, Tony returned a revised appraisal, approved by Robert, in which my performance was rated "outstanding." This incident provides a compelling example of the difference between white and black attitudes concerning the same set of facts. I felt I had to fight for justice in the face of unfair treatment. Tony let everyone know that he felt he had done me a big favor.

At the time, I was the only black professional man in a regional office. While I had purposely never raised the issue, I believed the state of race relations in the whole Office of Ocean and Coastal Resources Management was most unfortunate. A black professional woman named Kim, who was a GS-12 official on Edward's staff, met with me to discuss office discrimination. She was knowledgeable of my experiences and those of several other blacks in the office. Alert, aggressive and unobtrusively assertive, Kim suggested that we go together to Edward, in his capacity as chief, to discuss the race problems directly. I agreed.

During our meeting, Edward did not express a defensive attitude. He simply said he had never noticed any racial issues or problems in the office. To Kim's and my contrary assertions, he responded by asking us to cite specific examples. Kim related the case of a black woman who had talked to Tony about applying for a certain position and that Tony had advised against it because it would have necessitated her taking a down-grade from a GS-9 to a GS-7. Based on this advice, the black woman did not apply. Tony then hired a white woman for the job and gave it a GS-9 rating. We also pointed out many instances where white employees had convened critical work-related meetings without including black staff members who should have been included. I related several of the Mary and Betty incidents which provided clear evidence of racially discriminatory conduct. We talked about many other incidents and did our best to convince Edward that management needed to be more sensitive to racial matters and work to build an office attitude intolerant of prejudice.

Edward was entirely unmoved by our allegations or our suggestions. He said nothing in response and took no action after the meeting. Obviously, he was entirely satisfied with the state of race relations in his domain.

Once Bert had settled into his job, I decided to seek other opportunities in the office. My relationship with Bert was fine, but I didn't need to put up with Mary and Betty's attitude any longer. More importantly, it was without question that I was not going any further in the Pacific Region. One of the positions I applied for was that of a program analyst, or evaluator, in another division. This position would require me to evaluate programs in Edward and Tony's area of direct supervision, so my cup of optimism was not overflowing.

To my surprise, Tony selected me for the position and I was promoted to GS-13. While I was quite pleased to have new challenges and the upgrade, I did my best to avoid recognizing that both Edward and Tony wanted to put Mary and Betty on a promotional fast track, but couldn't do it with me in the Pacific Region because my seniority would have blocked their rise.

My new supervisor, a white woman named Alice who had a master's degree in business administration and had been in the office almost from its creation, was known for her aversion to confrontations and had a reputation for finding a way to diplomatically resolve conflicts. During the first two evaluations I performed, there were problems between myself and Edward's staff concerning some of my conclusions. Alice supported the staff and not me. I knew that, in the future, I would have to defend myself.

At staff meetings, Alice, on several occasions, showed disinterest with my presentations by cutting me off and allowing other white staff members to ramble on when giving their presentations. She hired young, white employees so she could control them and frequently gave them timely promotions and awards.

Sylvia was a white regional manager who had also been in the office from the beginning. She had a reputation for being verbally abusive with a "know-it-all" attitude. I first encountered her during an incident when I was acting regional manager. She had encouraged her friend, Mary, not to complete a task I had assigned. At my insistence, Mary grudgingly completed the assignment, but Sylvia never lessened her interference in my regional management. It was inevitable that in my new position, I would have to work with Sylvia again.

The first encounter was not long in coming. Before I left for a trip I knew would include Sylvia, Tony held a meeting of all evaluators and their supervisors. His main point was he felt the regional managers and their staffs were taking over evaluations and putting their own spins on them. He wanted evaluators to seize back the initiative and exert legitimate control over the evaluation process.

The following week, Sylvia and I went on a trip to Pennsylvania, one of the states in her region that was under evaluation. I had previously sent everyone, including Sylvia, an agenda for the meeting. From the opening of the meeting, Sylvia took control and led the discussions on other topics without regard to the evaluation agenda I had circulated. During a break, I asked her to follow the agenda and not deviate to unrelated subjects. She was obviously furious, but she complied. Sometime later in the day, she called Edward and complained that I was preventing her from speaking at the meeting. She added two more direct lies: that I asked the state program manager and his staff not to speak; and that the meeting was in a state of total confusion because of my actions.

Two weeks later, I learned that Sylvia had also coerced a white, state program manager to call Alice and complain about my performance. Sylvia frequently exercised power over state officials by threatening to deny funds or delay projects. I was able to get Alice to support me on the complaint because she couldn't deny Tony's new policy for evaluators to take charge of the process.

An important part of the evaluation process is timeliness. Before any program evaluation begins, the program analyst and his supervisor jointly work out a time schedule for orderly completion of the work. Alice and I did this prior to all evaluations, including the evaluation for the state of Pennsylvania. Everyone understood that these parameters were requisite to orderly work scheduling. I provided a draft evaluation report to Sylvia including the date for her to return it to me with her comments. She ignored the return deadline and withheld the document for many days afterward. When I finally received her comments, they were petty and she made many unwarranted changes. I could see no reason for the inordinate delay and bogus comments, except to embarrass me. After several strained meetings with Sylvia, I made some minor changes and the evaluation, including all my original recommendations, was accepted by the state manager.

Sylvia did not limit her supply of racial venom to Eric Hughes. Everyone of color knew that he or she would become her target at some point. Louis, one of the two black managers in the national program, was prepared when she went after him. At an important national conference, Sylvia announced that Louis had failed to submit certain information to her. He insisted that he had sent it and that he had done so on time. In point of fact, she had simply misplaced the information, but became furious at Louis' rebuttal. He responded by producing his copy of the memorandum which carried a dated receipt carrying Sylvia's initials.

Sometimes her accusations were wild. The population of the U.S. Virgin Islands is almost totally African-American. The only meetings where Sylvia claimed that federal funds may have been used to launder drugs were ones where these islands were under discussion. She never offered any possible reason or evidence for these assertions and a program audit never found any evidence of misuse of funds. But nothing stopped Sylvia's wrath.

Sylvia was a visible and vocal bigot. More will be heard about her later on in this narrative, but my job also required enduring the routine rejections black people in America face when it is necessary to function in the white world. Before any state meeting on program evaluation, I would circulate a proposed agenda for comment, carry on many telephone conversations with participants about the upcoming meeting and have several information exchanges by fax and mail. They knew who I was and that I was in charge of the evaluation. But at every meeting, the white state officials would overlook me and address their questions to my white colleagues, whom I outranked. I never ceased being amazed at my perceived invisibility while attending state meetings.

When a state is to be evaluated, a notice usually appears in the local newspaper advertising a public meeting concerning the coastal program. Almost always, the attendees were all white. With few exceptions, newspaper reporters at the meetings would seek out my white co-workers for interviews, never imagining that the only black person present would be the federal team leader.

After working two years as an evaluator, I noticed that a regional manager vacancy had been posted. Since this was a position under Edward's direct supervision, I knew my selection would be doubtful. While we both maintained a proper and professional relationship, there was little doubt in my mind that he didn't like blacks, in general, and me in particular. On the other hand, I knew of no one in the office more qualified and I wanted the promotion. So, I applied. The personnel officer who screened my application marked it "highly qualified" and sent it to Edward for an interview.

Immediately afterward, Tony notified the personnel office to suspend the vacancy announcement and said he would let them know when he wanted it re-posted. A month later, the position was re-posted and Tony, as selecting official, awarded the position to Jack, the same person who had yelled in the hallways that the free ride for blacks was over.

Jack had not applied for the vacancy on the first posting and had never served as an acting regional manager. Jack had been the only applicant responding to the second posting and had cited Edward as a job reference.

I met with Tony about not getting the promotion. He would only say that he had selected the best person for the job. I then told him in strong terms that I did not agree and asked him to reconsider. He suggested that I not make problems in the office because I might need a job reference in the future which he would not provide if I continued complaining. In closing the meeting, he said that he could make my life miserable in the office and that I should just get over it.

Tony's statement and attitude were infuriating. But by the time I got home to discuss the subject with Norma, I had calmed down enough to be rational. We talked about my growing desire to file a formal complaint. She was not surprised because we routinely discussed what was going on in each other's offices. In her position as human resource adviser in another part of NOAA, she told me about numerous injustices to African-Americans in regard to denied promotions, awards and assignments. In her former positions as chair of the Equal Employment Committee and Upward Mobility Program counselor, she told me about the reluctance of white managers to accept African-American professionals into their offices and the delays in promoting them once they were in the positions. We knew that my situation mirrored these injustices. I was concerned that any action of mine might adversely affect her, professionally. But we decided that it wouldn't, and even if it did, she still supported me fully.

We also discussed how we struggled to send our oldest daughter, Tracy, to college during the State Department case. This time our youngest daughter, Wendy, was a sophomore in college. But we agreed that to endure any financial hardships would be worth the struggle.

Only two years had passed since my victory over the State's discrimination. I knew full well the years and agony that were required to forcefully pursue a formal complaint. I also knew that, unlike my battle with State, I would have to remain in the same office which I was fighting for the entire duration of the war. And it would be a war. It's not a prospect anyone wants to face. The easiest way would be to roll over and be quiet for several years remaining to retirement. I certainly didn't look forward to more years of continuous hassle. At the same time, I couldn't rid myself of life-long principles. If any one of us refuses to fight for justice, none of us will get it. If we're not willing to help destroy racial discrimination with our own personal refusal to tolerate it, can we retain the right to hate it? My intellect urged me to let it go – it wasn't worth it and I didn't need it. But my heart told me what had to be done.

CHAPTER SIX

On January 21, 1988, I filed a racial and sexual discrimination complaint against NOAA based upon my non-selection to the regional manager position. Again, Attorney June Kalijarvi agreed to take my case. We raised numerous discrimination instances and conditions in the workplace in our filing. We knew we would drop these later on and concentrate on the non-selection issue. But we needed to include them in order to establish the discriminatory office environment in which the non-selection took place.

The agency Equal Employment Opportunity resolution counselor met with Edward and Tony to discuss my complaint. Their stand was that I had not been treated differently than anyone else and, therefore, no discrimination had occurred. They also asserted that no retaliation would take place as a result of my filing that complaint. Tony mentioned that he had promoted me and that I was letting paranoid tendencies cloud the facts. They evidenced every confidence that they would prevail and pointed to Jack's numerous outstanding performance appraisals. Of course, all of their office favorites received such ratings without regard to actual work achievements, but that had yet to be introduced and proven. After several meetings with the two of them, the counselor completed her review and asked Edward and Tony if they would consider settling the case. They refused to consider the option and rejected any discussions which might lead to settlement. This ended the preliminary rounds and triggered a formal investigation of my filing.

The first action the director and deputy director took was to ignore their promise of no retaliation against me for having filed the complaint. Since I was still there working everyday in the office, it amazed me that they thought the blatancy of their next actions would escape my observation. They sought out staff members who had worked with me over the years and directed them to make up lists of instances when I hadn't done my job and, in many cases, to tell outright lies. They presented a list of nine people in addition to themselves that they wanted the investigator to interview. There were several managers who had never worked with me and the list contained two state agency people whom they alleged had complained to the office about my performance. Since their power over state officials was tantamount to professional life and death because of the ease with which they could delay or deny federal funds, I was surprised that they could only produce two who were willing to parrot their line.

The product of their arrogance was shortsightedness. Two of the regional managers on their list, Milton and Irene, had been supervisors of Kim, the black professional whom I had earlier joined with in an informal attempt to get Edward to recognize the pervasiveness of racial discrimination in the office and to institute sensitivity programs to counter it. When Kim had been on Milton's staff, she had been the most experienced coastal management person in his region. Her personnel file bulged with proof that she was good at what she did. But Milton continually harassed all his black employees and particularly singled out Kim as his target. As is so often the case with supervisory discrimination, Kim found it more expedient to transfer out of his sphere than endure his constant slights. Irene was another manager who spent considerable time in meetings belittling any programs managed by black or other minority personnel. Her North Atlantic Region had no programs managed by a minority state official. Unlike Sylvia, who always opposed the black state official, Irene was smart enough to openly attack only the programs themselves. She consistently voted in meetings to turn down projects that would have benefited areas such as Puerto Rico, Hawaii and the U.S. Virgin Islands.

By this time, Kim, believing that Irene was a fair manager, had transferred to Irene's region, a move she later would regret. Irene mistreated Kim by placing unreasonable deadlines on her work tasks. Unfortunately, after Milton and then Irene, there was nowhere for Kim to go. She had to endure the mistreatment for several more years. Eventually, Irene left the agency and Kim performed with minimal harassment from her new supervisor.

When I read Edward and Tony's initial affidavits in the investigation phase of the case, it became clear that they had abandoned the traditional defense against a racial discrimination complaint. Normally, managers in such situations compiled every possible bit of evidence to prove that their actions were unbiased in any manner. Such efforts always concentrated on attempts to prove consistent even-handedness and impartiality in every action. While their testimonies referenced some supportive material, they abandoned the high ground of trying to prove that they had managed the office in a manner promoting relational homeostasis among employees to take the lower road of attacking and attempting to destroy Eric Hughes. Tony said that my case was unworthy of his time, that my capabilities were limited and that my competence was below that necessary for federal service above my current grade level. Edward said that I hadn't the knowledge to do the work and lacked the interpersonal skills to supervise a professional staff. They both alleged having received complaints from office staffers and state officials that I had done a bad job of evaluating programs. Their witnesses' affidavits generally supported these personal deficiency claims but did not reflect the venom contained in Edward and Tony's recitations.

The main reason why racial discrimination cases are so very difficult to prove is because in the end, the testimony of witnesses becomes paramount. Unless a manager has written something monumentally stupid (and neither Edward nor Tony was stupid) the most meaningful evidentiary material rests on the statements of those who were there. Unlike civil or criminal trials, the witnesses in a discrimination case are, by force of circumstance, almost always under the daily supervision and control of the accused managers. Since those who stand in defense of their actions have career advancement power over everyone they call to speak on their behalf, they can erect a wall of subtly coerced falsehoods which will weaken the resolve of a complainant's witnesses or intimidate them from coming forward at all. Who is going to stand up and openly testify against someone who thereafter will remain in control of their daily lives for years to come?

In my case, the managers in question were known to act according to their whims rather than policy; their reputations for promoting friends and ignoring everyone else were firmly established; and their proclivity for retaliation was a matter of general knowledge. I found only one employee, Kim, who was willing to aim her lance at my chosen windmill. Fortunately, I was also able to muster two additional witnesses who were no longer under the control of Edward and Tony.

Bert's affidavit affirmed that my performance as acting regional manager had been entirely competent, that I had good skills and worked well with others. He pointed out that the Pacific Region was the most difficult region to manage and that, when he had taken it over from me, it was in good shape. When asked to summarize, he said that I was hardworking, responsible and dedicated. He also added that Edward and Tony discriminated against African-Americans, in general, and exhibited a particular animus toward me. Kim and my other witness, a black secretary who had transferred out of the office to another agency, offered testimony which supported my claim of a discriminatory office environment by citing numerous examples of management misconduct.

As is almost pro forma in the early stages of cases such as mine, the defending agency, NOAA, issued a finding of no discrimination and moved to dismiss the case. In other words, my agency declared itself not guilty. This allowed me to move beyond the judgment of my own superiors and petition for a hearing before an independent agency, EEOC.

During the months of the investigative process and for the period leading up to the agency declaring itself innocent, I worked in the office under the required presumption that business should go on as before without retaliation. This was supposed to continue for the year or so it would take for my hearing to be scheduled and for whatever additional time was required for a ruling after the hearing.

As a practical matter, it would be impossible to maintain a normal work atmosphere in any organization where a very public and lengthy battle was going on between a professional staff member and his two top managers. People are human and cannot resist the temptation to take sides or to express themselves. White staff members who had been previously cordial to me now avoided eye contact and passed me silently in the hallways. Many whites were simply afraid to be seen in my company for fear word would get back to Edward and Tony. Conversations were held in whispers when I came near. It serves no major purpose here to go into a dissertation on these day-to-day exclusions or to dwell on the inner strength it took to put up with them for so many months. It can help one's understanding of my situation, however, to bring out some instances of management retaliation that were major enough to affect my case.

It was common knowledge that since Tony announced he would be leaving the office within several months, he had been working on ways to get his two favorite white women promoted. Things like "common knowledge" can never be proved, but it does tend to make one watchful for events that can be substantiated.

During the time after filing my complaint there were bulletin board postings for two GS-14 vacancies in the office. One was for a position newly established by Tony and duly approved by the personnel office for a supervisory policy and program analyst. The other post was for that of a regional manager. I sent off applications for both positions and my paperwork came back marked "highly qualified." Tony was thereby almost required to grant me a selection interview, even though everyone in the office knew that he had created the new position in order to promote a white woman named Shelly and had pre-selected Mary for the regional manager's position. Both women were appointed to the advertised positions and Eric Hughes was passed over again.

My lawyer and I believed that enough evidence existed to prove that my non-selection to either of the vacancies was in direct retaliation for my having filed the initial complaint. Tony's original affidavit provided sufficient indication of his feelings toward me, so we filed another discrimination complaint against him and asked that it be consolidated with my existing filing.

Our new filings set out the facts that Shelly and I had both worked as GS-13's in the evaluation unit prior to the vacancy posting, but that I had worked with more states, served for nearly a year as acting regional manager and had considerable seniority over her. In addition, affirmative action guidelines indicated that, since there were no minority GS-14's anywhere in the office, fully qualified minorities should be afforded an edge.

Shelly had been selected despite the fact that she had been absent from the office attending school for approximately 85 percent of the time, Monday through Friday, during the 18 months prior to her promotion over me. Even the 15 percent of the time she was supposed to have been in the office was doubtful because her schedule called for her to be in the office from 2:30 until 4:30 every afternoon, but she had rarely been seen there. The government had paid, on Tony's approval, about $9,000 for her classes and parking. I noticed that our new white supervisor, Bud, would open her office door every day and turn on the lights to make it appear that she was at work, but away from her desk. Since Bud was not on Tony's list of preferred people (Tony often demeaned him and publicly called him derogatory names), I assumed that he covered for Shelly on Tony's orders.

Upon learning about my second complaint, Shelly handed the secretary a backdated schedule indicating that she had been in the office between the hours of 11:45 and 4:30 every afternoon Wednesdays and Fridays. This transparent attempt at track-covering resulted in the existence of two conflicting schedules for the same time period.

Other people in the office had complained anonymously to the department's inspector general about Shelly's favored treatment, continuous absence from work over many months and the lack of any relationship between the courses she was taking and her work. The Office of Inspector General chose to not take notice of the favoritism allegations, but did investigate all records concerning her academic pursuits during working hours. A ruling was soon sent down that, in the future, any outside training requested by Shelly be done on her own non-working hours and be paid for with her own funds.

Shortly after Shelly had been promoted to the new supervisory policy and program analyst position that Tony had created, he abolished the position and created another one in the Sanctuaries and Reserves Division at the GS-14 level. With this move of lateral transfer, he positioned her for later promotions.

When the investigator of my second complaint took Tony's affidavit, he made special note in his report that throughout the interview, Tony made repeated disparaging remarks about me and frequently called me an "idiot" and "stupid." When the investigator mentioned during the interview that I had alleged he had a personal relationship with Shelly, Tony responded that I would "fry" for that remark. Tony ended his affidavit by admitting that he had selected Shelly without getting a recommendation from her supervisor and that he had not relied on her performance appraisals. He claimed that he had made his selection based solely on her qualifications, training, experience and ability to do the job.

Mary's favored treatment was only slightly less egregious than Shelly's. Some time after I had left the Pacific Region, Tony transferred Mary to the South Atlantic and Gulf Region. His two reasons were clear to any observer of office politics. He wanted her in a position where she and Betty would not be in competition with each other and he had future promotions in mind for her. About six months later, Tony asked the personnel office to reclassify and revise the job descriptions for the positions Mary and Betty then held. As soon as this request was approved, he promoted both of them to the new classification, GS-13. Later on, he split the South Atlantic and Gulf Region into two separate units. This left Mary acting as Gulf regional manager and Jack held on to the level he gained from his promotion over me and was now regional manager of the new South Atlantic Region.

The obvious final step in this convoluted trail of favoritism was to get Mary promoted to the permanent position of regional manager. This was the point at which Tony left the office and a white man named Warren was appointed to his place. When Edward asked the personnel office to advertise a vacancy for the position of Gulf regional manager, Warren knew nothing of the history behind the act. Kim and I both applied for the newly posted position. We each had five years seniority over Mary and I had been her supervisor for ten months. In an objective world of promotion based on merit and experience, either of us would easily have been chosen over Mary.

Edward had Warren join him in the selection process with Edward being the recommending official and Warren being the selecting official. No one in the office was surprised that Warren selected Mary for the promotion.

Shortly after Mary's promotion announcement, we passed each other in the hall. She let out a loud utterance that could have been interpreted as a snicker, but was to me an insulting derisive sneer of victory over Kim and I. This tasteless exhibition and attempt to embarrass me was a personal provocation I probably could not have overlooked from a man. In Mary's case, my anger hardened into resolve.

My complaint concerning being passed over for promotion in the case of Mary's ascendancy was investigated by another interview and affidavit process. Both Warren and Edward were interviewed. But since Warren had no prior knowledge of events leading up to the promotion, he could not offer much except a statement that Mary was the best candidate of the three. Edward stated that I lacked strong substantive knowledge of the program and had difficulty getting along with people. He alleged that it had been necessary for him to resolve disputes between me and other office staff. He also claimed to have had complaints about my work performance from state officials whose programs I had evaluated. Finally, he stated that my outstanding performance rating came about because I was improving and not because I maintained that level of performance.

As time went on, my interaction with the state officials was increasingly affected. They could not help but hear office gossip. Some were sympathetic and others meticulously avoided the topic. I could usually tell which ones Edward had called to solicit negative comments about me because they became the most distant and unwilling to talk with me even about their own programs. The minor retaliations at work continued with supervisors delaying return of my documents so that I would always be behind in my work schedule and a diminishing willingness of white professionals to cooperate when we had to work together on parts of evaluations. There was little I could do except to continue producing errorless work and showing no outward emotions.

My time will come, I told myself, when the truth comes out at the hearing.

CHAPTER SEVEN

The formal hearing was set for February 24, 1989, at Commerce headquarters building. It is in downtown Washington on the east-side of a public park behind the White House, known simply as the Ellipse because of its geometrical shape.

I arrived early that day and went to the cafeteria for a light breakfast. What I encountered, if somehow depicted in photographic form, could have become a compelling graphic telling the whole story of a black person fighting racial discrimination in the federal government. At one table, Eric Hughes sat alone nursing his coffee and donuts until the appropriate hour. Not far from him, two tables had been pulled together and surrounded by 11 white civil servants speaking in hushed voices as Edward and Tony coached the other nine in the tactics to be employed that day in the attempted destruction of someone who had the audacity to challenge their inbred bias. There was no photographer on the ceiling to take such a picture, but the imagery of the scene is one that will never leave my mind.

The hearing room was smaller than I had imagined, about ten by 16 feet. A long table was centered in the room. The presiding administrative judge, a well-dressed black woman sitting at the head of the table, evidenced a pleasant-enough attitude while also speaking in a manner leaving no doubt that she was firmly in charge of the proceedings. To her left, the government's attorney, a bald, white man of middle-age and indeterminate manner, sat silently. My attorney and I were seated to the administrative judge's right. An empty chair for witnesses sat to the left of the government's attorney facing me. This was going to be up close and personal.

My experience with June's representation of me at the end of my State case had taught me that her short stature and almost fragile physical appearance provided excellent camouflage for a hardline aggressive style and served to hide her long experience in employment discrimination cases. We worked well together and were fully prepared for the hearing.

Both sides had previously submitted documents they felt would contribute to the record. My lawyer and I had previously contacted several state program managers I had evaluated over the years to see if they would be witnesses for me. Fear of reprisal against their programs prevented any of them from actually stepping forward on my behalf. Two of them, both black, wrote letters that I had been both competent and fair. We had not submitted these letters with our other documents because we wanted to use them in rebuttal if the testimony justified their introduction.

We had only three witnesses to call: Bert, the man appointed to regional manager when I had been passed over for promotion to that office; Kim, who was my only witness who still worked in the office; and another black woman, Sarah, who had transferred out of Commerce to escape the continuous discrimination by Edward and Tony. Thus, the ratio of government witnesses to the four of us would be nearly three to one. Bert was the first to take the chair.

He gave his testimony with a confident demeanor and professional attitude. He affirmed that when he took over the region which I had been managing for ten months, he encountered no languishing problems and found the office in good shape. He went on to say that I exhibited no resentment or animosity toward him because he had replaced me in the position and that he soon came to rely on me and to regard me as a valuable member of his staff.

When my attorney asked him to discuss Jack, Bert responded with the opinion that Jack was a competent professional, but that he did not evidence either my initiative or hard work ethic. When pushed for a characterization, Bert said that Jack placed his own interests above those of his job. When asked who was the better-qualified employee for the promotion, Bert said that both Jack and I were comparable on levels of ability and knowledge, but that he would have given me the promotion because I would have been the more conscientious and devoted to the job.

When the testimony turned to his interpretation of Tony, Bert's comments became more biting. Tony, in his opinion, ran the office as though it was his personal playground. He made decisions based on no more than whatever moved him at the moment. He favored those employees he liked with privileges, promotions and awards while ignoring all others. When asked, specifically, about racial attitudes, Bert stated plainly that blacks were never included in Tony's consideration and that he was convinced Tony had discriminated against me, based only on race, in many matters.

Edward, in Bert's opinion, was not a notable manager and moved to address problems only after they rose to a critical level, rather than taking early action to prevent them. Edward usually deferred to Tony with regard to personnel matters and promotions. When my attorney asked him for specificity concerning racial attitudes, Bert replied that whenever the name Eric Hughes came up in conversations, Edward would exhibit personal annoyance.

When asked about Mary and Betty, he reported that they resented me and did not like working for me. Bert said that he, too, had problems trying to manage Mary and Betty because they were both headstrong and hated having their work reviewed by anyone other than Tony or Edward. Even though they were under his direct management supervision, Mary and Betty would always go around Bert to Tony with any of their problems.

Bert described the incident of my performance appraisal shortly after he became regional manager. Since he had little experience with me at that time, he asked Edward for input. Edward told him to give me a mediocre rating, but would not offer any reasons. Bert decided to give me a commendable rating, then described my protest to Tony and the rating's subsequent upgrading to outstanding. Bert pointed out that Eric Hughes had not been the only member of his staff subjected to performance appraisal interference by Edward and Tony. He testified that Tony twice had ordered him to give Mary, Bud and Betty outstanding ratings. If he refused, Tony said he would, as reviewing official, change them himself. Bert had carried out the orders.

When shown Tony's affidavit from the investigative phase, Bert strongly disagreed with the characterizations of me being unworthy of promotion and incapable of competent federal service beyond my current level. He reported that both Edward and Tony routinely took complaints from Mary and Betty as important, but always labeled me as a troublemaker and never evidenced interest in anything I had to say.

Bert's summary testimony was the best I could have imagined.

He characterized Edward and Tony as managers who promoted people entirely on the basis of a candidate's personal loyalty to them and without regard to seniority, experience or ability to perform. They did this, in Bert's opinion, because they wanted to exert total and absolute personal control over every penny of the entire $40 million in annual grants. Their method of doing this was to exclusively hire and promote people upon whose unquestioned loyalty they could depend. Since they had no black friends and never felt comfortable dealing with black people, no black employee ever had the slightest chance of advancement under the sole criteria of personal loyalty being the basis for any transfer, promotion or award. Bert's concluding observation was that Edward and Tony consistently discriminated against blacks in general and against Eric Hughes in particular.

Kim, who had been my co-worker for seven years, gave testimony that dwelled on the general racial discriminatory atmosphere in the office. She was qualified to present evidence on the subject because she had served on the office Equal Employment Opportunity Committee for some years and had served as chairwoman for a year. For four years, she had represented the director of our office on the committee. In this capacity, she had been designated as the individual to provide the director with suggestions and ideas on how to improve equal opportunity for minorities within the unit.

According to Kim, the main thrust of the committee suggestions had been on how to improve recruiting practices to attract more blacks and other minorities. My lawyer asked why this had been the top priority. Kim responded by saying that of the 80 employees in the unit, there were five blacks, all women, who served in clerical jobs and seven black professionals, of whom only one, Eric Hughes, was male. No black professional served at any grade level above GS-13. While the minority ratio for the office was 15 percent, the ratio for professionals was less than 10 percent. With such a low ratio of blacks to whites, the committee felt that recruiting African-American professionals should be the first order of business.

In speaking about the general atmosphere, Kim provided data which supported her statement that whites, as a group, were promoted faster and higher than blacks. She also added that every black employee in the office felt performance expectations for blacks were higher than for whites. One example she provided was that of a white woman on the staff who was a chronic complainer and who rarely submitted satisfactory work products. These things would have resulted in discipline for an African-American, yet the worst performance rating she had ever received was that of "commendable."

Kim's testimony about upper management support of African-American supervisors mirrored my experience. When she had been acting regional manager, Edward had encouraged certain members of her staff to undercut her and come directly to him with their problems. He would also override her performance ratings. It was as if management felt African-American supervisors didn't exist. In this connection, Kim described the sensitivity meeting she and I held with Edward in an effort to improve office race relations and the fact he had been completely unresponsive.

Kim also described a casual conversation she shared with Jack. Apparently they had come together in the parking lot on the way to their cars and were chatting innocuously when Jack said something to the effect, "Well, you know Eric. He's always complaining...always hollering discrimination. If he doesn't get what he wants or doesn't get the job, the first thing he'll do is holler discrimination." Then Jack had asked her, "But don't you think that you've been treated fairly? Don't you think that, you know, the treatment is equal as far as you are concerned?" After suffering daily discrimination in the office for so many years, it was all Kim could do to walk away without screaming at him.

I could not help asking myself how Jack could accuse me of hollering anything after his hallway demonstration in the wake of Reagan's election.

My final witness was a young, black woman named Sarah, who had managed a transfer out of the department. She had been a GS-3 physical science aid in our office. At the time of her first incident with Edward, she had set up and conducted a computer training program for senior level staff and had solved office computer problems no one else could figure out. When she first approached Edward for a promotion, he said he couldn't promote her because her job title was not on any career ladder. Edward later changed her job title to clerk-typist and when Sarah again mentioned the possibility of promotion, he denied the possibility due to her title. Knowing that her title was on a career ladder, Sarah waited awhile and then brought the subject of promotion up one more time. Edward responded that her work was not up to par.

Sarah stated that this discrimination was race-based since a white man who had preceded her in the same tasks had been promoted to a GS-7 when the promotion she was asking for was that of a GS-4.

As the selecting official accused of racial discrimination, Tony was the first of the government witnesses. Even though all government witnesses sat directly across the table from me at a distance of about three feet, neither Tony nor any of the others ever made eye contact with me during the hearing.

Tony opened with a gratuitous comment that he had gone out of his way to get me the temporary promotion when I had been selected acting regional manager. When asked about the position in question, he simply stated that Jack was better qualified. Pushed a little by my attorney for more information, he added that he had also had problems with me and that he had once mediated a dispute between two divisions over an issue in my evaluation document which should have been resolved at my level. He then cited general problems with me, such as underperformance, inability to get along with people in the office and, more importantly, a lack of real in-depth knowledge of the program. He even parroted the unctuous statement in his affidavit that I was unworthy of promotion and incapable of competent federal service beyond my current level.

My attorney then led him through testimony concerning his having raised my performance rating from commendable to outstanding. His first response was a flip comment saying that since he had expected nothing from me, anything would have rated outstanding. She then asked about each of the elements which can lead to an outstanding rating and, by the time she was through with him, Tony had admitted that performance appraisals (including Jack's) meant nothing to him. Before leaving the stand, he admitted that he had never recommended or promoted any black employee above the level of GS-13.

Several times during his testimony Tony tried to interrupt my attorney to make a point. Each time the administrative judge had to admonish him to be quiet and not speak until asked.

As Tony finally departed the room even the administrative judge, a model of impartiality, was shaking her head.

As the complainant, my testimony came next. Since much of this book has been spent setting out the events that led to the hearing, there is no need to restate them at length again here. I offered proof by example of how favored white employees were promoted almost annually and blacks almost never. At one point, I was asked if Tony's testimony came as a surprise to me. I answered in the affirmative. I said I was surprised by his attacks regarding my performance, my capabilities and by his denial of discriminating against me. The very next question from the government's attorney was if I had been surprised by Edward's affidavit. I said no. By the time of his affidavit he had already convinced me, by word and deed, that he instinctively acted with racial bias. His recitations affirming it were no surprise.

Mary and Betty testified next. Their testimonies were almost interchangeable. In effect, they claimed I was a non-communicative bully with an overbearing management style. Both admitted that they had never before been supervised by a black person and denied that I had been a victim of discrimination.

Milton's testimony was fairly typical of that espoused by the team Edward and Tony had assembled with the attempt to destroy me. He started out confident to an extent bordering on arrogance and recited the list of sins that had been alleged by Tony. His exuberance to join in the kill, however, must have overcome whatever trace of judgment he possessed because he told two lies. The first one was that a staff professional, a black female who had sometimes worked with me, expressed her concerns to him that I was not adequately preparing for the evaluation of the Alabama Coastal Management Program. Milton went on to say that her observations had been justified in that my evaluation of that state had brought complaints from the Alabama state program manager saying my evaluation had been shallow and weak. My attorney handed Milton a letter which I had previously arranged to be sent to her and asked him to read it into the record. He was thus forced to read aloud the following words from the Alabama state program manager: "There were periods during the evaluation process when we disagreed with Mr. Hughes on several coastal issues, but overall his assessment and evaluation were comprehensive, sound and virtually devoid of political assertions."

Edward was smarter than Milton and limited his testimony to matters of allegation and judgment which were always the most difficult sort of assertions to disprove. He said he had gone out of his way to get me a temporary promotion to GS-13 when I had become acting regional manager. It wasn't true, but who could prove it? When my attorney asked him about his having asked to do the appraisals on two white women while telling me to do the same for a black woman, he simply replied that he knew much more about the performance of Mary and Betty and less about the unit secretary and was therefore justified in handling the matter the way he did. He went on to allege complaints from my staff concerning my communication problems and tendency to bully rather than lead. He also claimed to have received complaints during my evaluations of two coastal programs that claimed I lacked substantive knowledge of the programs.

In his response to my attorney's questions, he admitted that these complaints from the two states had not been mentioned in his affidavit and affirmed that I had received outstanding ratings for supervisory and administrative functions. His parting statement was that he would not have recommended me for a GS-14 position anywhere in the office and if Jack had not applied for the position in question, he still would not have recommended me for it.

Of the remaining government witnesses, only Sylvia, who testified last, had comments beyond rote repetition of the party line concerning my alleged program incompetence and inability to get along with people. She brought up the conference where I would not let her dominate and claimed I would not let her and some state officials speak at the meeting. She said I frightened her and that when she called Edward to report I had ordered her to remain silent, he told her to comply. She then added I was generally unprepared for most meetings and did not seem to understand the issues under discussion.

My attorney asked Sylvia if she had been aware Tony had set a new policy, just before the meeting in question, which required evaluators to be more aggressive in controlling meetings and to stick to the agendas. Sylvia replied she had not known of it.

As was my right under the hearing procedures, I was called as the final witness. I explained all the aspects of the meeting Sylvia had brought up and, in addition to covering the policy change, talked about how Sylvia, generally, tried to dominate meetings by taking over apparent leadership. My point in this testimony was that in a meeting of a dozen white people and one black, the whites would never assume the black was the leader. In fact, they always assumed that whichever white official from Washington talked first and most, was in charge. To adhere to the agenda, I had to assert myself as the person in charge or lose control by default. I ended refutation of her testimony by citing several examples of Sylvia delaying my reports and making constant minor, negative comments on them for the purpose of making my work product late.

By the end of my testimony, I had responded to every allegation of the government witnesses concerning legitimate reference to my work and office relationships. For instance, I went to some length concerning Milton's offhanded statement that I did a poor job in setting up agendas for evaluation trips and meetings. Looking directly at the administrative judge, I calmly recited each step of the procedure to emphasize the long communication and coordination process necessary for an evaluator to reach consensus between the state and federal official before each meeting on what the agenda should contain and what we were trying to achieve at any conference.

Perhaps the most important question was the last one my attorney put to me. She asked if, at any time during the years in question, anyone in authority had ever discussed with me matters such as my lack of program knowledge, deficient interpersonal skills, poor work product, or similar complaints about my professional conduct. At last, I could tell the world by a simple honest declarative response through the utterance of two words. I said, "No. Never."

With that statement, the hearing closed. During the ten hours of testimony, I had strived to remain alert at all times so that I would miss nothing and remain ready to help my attorney respond to every comment from nuance to outright lie. When the gavel closed the hearing, I was overcome with exhaustion and remained seated for awhile. My tiredness was not just physical. The emotional strain of sitting across from 11 people with whom I had worked every day for years and hearing them, from a distance of three feet, spend hour after hour assaulting my character, demeaning my knowledge, depreciating my achievements and, generally, denying my competence, had drained my soul.

The hardest part had been to just sit there and take it. Back in my military service days when a drunken, white airman on the bus poured out poisonous venom in my direction, I could at least respond with an immediate fist toward his nose. Now things were more civilized and orderly. Instead of epithets, insults were couched in polite phrases, lies told in reasonable tones and hatred disguised with a fig leaf of strained civility.

CHAPTER EIGHT

When I returned to work the next day, the office was literally buzzing with conversations about the hearing. The talk was not so much about the merits of my case, but about the facts of it. I was by no means the first African-American in NOAA to have suffered relentless racial discrimination at work. But I certainly was the first one in the Office of Ocean and Coastal Resources Management to have taken it all the way to adjudication. The typical response to the routine injustice faced by blacks was to avoid taking a public stand because of several fears. First, you are always vastly outnumbered, which is intimidating. Secondly, the prospect of work-related retaliation, both present and future, is terribly frightening. Finally, the expense, both emotional and financial, can be enormous since the strain of both costs will continue for years prior to any hope of resolution. So when my black co-workers were patting me on the back and the whites were huddled in debate about the case that day, I could only murmur to those willing to listen that we cannot end injustice by failing to oppose it.

I also knew the road ahead was still long and bumpy. My lawyer and I had 60 days to draft and submit final closing arguments to the administrative judge. We knew it would take a minimum of six months after our submission before her decision and recommended action would be handed down. We also strongly suspected that even if the decision was favorable to our cause, the department would appeal it.

I didn't have to wait very long for subtle retaliations to commence. It became increasingly difficult to get the necessary cooperation to do my job. Program evaluations, by their very nature, require input from several different levels of professional staff. In fact, it's not misleading to describe the evaluation process as that of assembling the views of various Washington staff officials and those of state program managers into a cohesive whole so that judgments can be made. By constantly clouding and delaying responses to my draft reports, Edward's staff quietly set out to sabotage my work product. Some of their efforts to thwart my job performance were transparently contrived to get me to explode. But I managed to suppress the urge. Providing my enemy with ammunition was not going to help anything.

In addition to work related retaliations, there were attempts to provoke me for other reasons. One day, for instance, a fellow worker who had never evidenced any taking of sides in my case, passed my desk and suggested that I go to the supply room and look at a fax which had been lying near the fax machine for some time. The supply room was a very public place because people frequented it regularly to make copies, send and receive faxes, obtain materials and often just to gossip. I went into the room and found a long fax concerning many sensitive facts about my pending case. There was no cover sheet revealing the name of sender or recipient. But the document was obviously part of real or contrived correspondence between attorneys for the government discussing points against me for possible use in closing arguments.

I took it and immediately called my attorney. She then sent a letter to the chief of the civil rights division complaining that it was utterly inappropriate in a sensitive equal employment opportunity case to fail to secure materials transmitted by facsimile machines. Since the contents seemed to have been designed to embarrass me and then left available for public inspection, she demanded an investigation.

There was a quick and, in our opinion, cursory investigation which concluded that the only person to have seen the fax was the one who told me about it. Since the fax had been sitting in public view for more than an hour in a high traffic location, this conclusion was ridiculous. But we were unable to get them to take any action.

After submitting closing arguments to the administrative judge, each side was provided with a copy of its opponent's documents.

We found no surprises in the government's recitations. They

continued to hang their case on the fact that favors had been done for me when I was selected as acting regional manager, which was meant to imply the action had been taken out of management largess rather than because I had earned it. It contained a rehash of all the allegations concerning my supposed underperformance and incompetence. The only thing added to known lies was a long section proclaiming the high virtues, impeccable credentials, rich experience, deep programmatic knowledge, excellent management skills and otherwise sterling character of their promotion selectee, Jack. Until reading this description of him, I hadn't realized that I had been in competition with a saint.

In our closing argument, we stressed the credibility of Bert's testimony as the only truly objective witness among those who had been or still were, one of my direct, senior supervisors because he no longer had anything to do with NOAA. We juxtaposed Bert's testimony concerning my competence and performance against the series of current management employees who had produced a litany of allegations about my supposed inadequacies without a single item of credible contemporaneous evidence to support them. To this, we turned their testimony against me to our favor by pointing out examples such as Tony's admission that performance appraisals meant nothing to him; and on Edward's insisting he appraise white employees under my supervision while demanding that I personally appraise the sole black employee on my staff.

My attorney also used much of the department's own data to support our assertion of an atmosphere of racial discrimination in employment opportunity throughout the office. She set out promotion data for a 28 month time frame during 1986 to 1988 which showed that of the 37 blacks promoted during the period, 92 percent had been for positions at GS-6 or below while 25 whites had been promoted with 70 percent of them upgraded to GS-9 and above positions. Further, 30 percent of these white promotions had been to grades GS-14 or 15. No black had ever received a promotion above GS-13. Data such as this, she asserted, not only documented significant minority under-representation in senior grades, but also led to the conclusion that they constitute stark evidence of a pattern of racial discrimination.

Initial victory finally came on November 13, 1989 when the administrative judge issued her decision that I had been a victim of racial discrimination on the issue of the denied promotion set out in my complaint. She recommended that I be promoted to GS-14 and be awarded back pay and attorneys' fees.

In her decision, the judge emphasized the fact that all of Edward's allegations concerning my communications problems, lack of program knowledge and inferior performance were verified nowhere in the evidence. She pointed out that none of my performance appraisals from 1985 through 1987, all of which had been signed by Edward, reflected any hint of these deficiencies.

She was even harder on Tony by stating her conclusion that his allegations against me and assertions in favor of Jack constituted a cover-up to hide the truth that his selection had been based on race. Since Tony claimed to have no interest in performance appraisals, including Jack's, his decision had to have been made subjectively. The evidence supported a conclusion that any subjective decision of his had to be race-based. She reviewed the entire matter of Tony halting the selection process when it was clear that I was the only qualified candidate and then re-opening the process when Jack had been pre-selected by Edward to fill the vacancy. Finally, she pointed out that Tony had signed my performance evaluations, which had noted none of his allegations of my deficiencies during the time period in question. Accordingly, he could not claim now what he had failed to record then.

Every word that got back to me about the decision led me to believe that the highest officials in our bureaucracy were both stunned and outraged by the administrative judge's opinion and recommended decision, even though the agency still had opportunities to oppose the recommended action.

Apparently, it was too much for them to live with because NOAA quickly opposed the recommended decision and issued its own final decision: that it could find no evidence its selection of another qualified candidate was due to my race. Disregarding the administrative judge's findings entirely, it declared the matter concluded in favor of itself.

Within the proscribed time limits, we filed an appeal to the Office of Review and Appeals of EEOC. In preparing this series of documents, my attorney set out a complete recapitulation of the facts of the case. She honed in on the premise that the administrative judge had based her finding and recommendation on her firsthand observations of the testimony and credibility of witnesses and the agency could hardly be free now to review this evidence again in order to reverse a conclusion for no better reason than it had gone against them. She also cited the judge's inclusion of the agency's own public data verifying that no blacks had ever been promoted to the grade level which had been denied me as a result of a racially biased promotion decision.

She reminded EEOC that the agency had admitted a prima facie case of discrimination by never disputing facts that the basis of the complaint was race: I met the posted qualifications of the position, I was not selected, and a white candidate was selected without any evidence presented to document reason for preference other than race.

CHAPTER NINE

When the Office of Review and Appeals issued its opinion in my case on March 20, 1990, I was overjoyed. It upheld the administrative judge's decision and ruled against the agency's appeal.

In many ways, it was also critical of the investigation held prior to the hearing. It cited, for instance, Tony having told the investigator that my claim was, "unworthy of my time to respond to." The opinion strongly reminded the agency that management officials alleged to have violated Title VII did not have the luxury of refusing to respond to charges because they deemed them "unworthy." They went on to cite other evidence that Tony had failed to follow regulations which require management, and especially upper-level management, to cooperate fully with an investigator of a discrimination complaint. The opinion went on to mention that Tony and Edward's stated reasons for not selecting me were suspect because they were not mentioned in the performance appraisals or investigation phases and were only introduced in the hearing itself. This raised the possibility that the reasons and the evidence supporting them were after-the-fact justifications to conceal a discriminatory action. Finally, they agreed with the judge's finding that there was strong evidence to suggest that Jack had been pre-selected. While pre-selection itself is not an arrangement of discrimination, it is relevant to discriminatory intent.

In the agency's appeal, they had asserted that management had the right to rely on subjective judgments based on personal observations. The review opinion dismissed this by stating that subjective factors used to evaluate promotion applications had been uniformly held by courts to be particularly susceptible to abuse and required close scrutiny.

The review opinion agreed with the agency's contention that it was not relevant whether the recommending official, Edward, and the selecting official, Tony, were correct in their assessments of my deficiencies; but only whether they believed that these deficiencies existed at the time of their selection decision. However, the review opinion found the weight of evidence simply would not support a finding that Tony and Edward had a good faith belief in these deficiencies.

There followed a lengthy list of each of the agency's articulated reasons for its actions in the case, followed by a specific statement of review denying the validity of each one. In the end, the conclusion that I had proven racial discrimination as the basis for my not getting the promotion rang true and clear. All that really mattered was that the final decision of the agency had been overruled in my favor.

Large, old-line government agencies, a characterization that certainly applies to Commerce, tend to become protective of the administrations, bureaus and units that make up the whole. At the top, there is almost always a "we can do no wrong" attitude. Such mindsets are surely institutional and are not aimed at any particular set of perceived enemies, but at any source of criticism which may come its way. A source of possible public announcement that the institution has done wrong is always neuralgic causing officials to blindly react in the same manner as a hawk protecting her chicks.

Rather than becoming a flag suggesting self-examination for the cause of the problem, EEOC's overturning of the department's final decision resulted in an immediate knee-jerk response to fight back. Commerce quickly filed a Request to Reopen. The name, Request to Reopen, is something of a misnomer. It is actually a final appeal. The only basis for an appeal such as this is a claim that the decision was wrong as a matter of law. No re-argument of the merits of the case or introduction of new evidence is permitted at this stage. The procedure is very much like a miniature Supreme Court hearing: two lawyers submit writings to a tribunal in which each explains why the other has misinterpreted the law of the land.

The department's Office of the General Counsel is headed by a presidentially appointed lawyer who not only has a large group of attorneys on his personal staff, but also commands the general counsel's offices in bureaus throughout the department. He or she thereby may be directly supported by hundreds of loyal lawyers. To oppose them in their appeal stood only one person, a slightly built, diminutive and bespectacled woman whose appearance could hardly be termed threatening: the attorney for Eric Hughes. I was the only one involved who knew that nothing intimidated her and no challenge could have pleased her more.

The problem faced by the high-powered lawyers who drafted the department's appeal was that no one on either side during the entire proceeding had tried to plow new legal fields. Neither side had developed nor introduced any new theory or esoteric interpretations of the law to justify a particular action or to support an item of evidence. With the legal envelope thus unstressed, it was not easy for them to challenge straight forward, even simple, interpretations of well-precedented civil rights law.

Their appeal therefore became a listing of facts with conclusions that could not be backed up with the usual citations of similar precedents established in similar cases. For instance, the appeals argued that pre-selection in a competitive promotion situation was not a violation of Title VII unless it was based upon consideration of prohibited discriminatory factors and concluded that the record did not support a finding that the agency's articulated reasons were false. At its root, such a claim is not truly an assertion of legal misinterpretation; no one would argue with their statement of law, but it's only an argument alleging evidential weakness.

In some instances, the appeal went so far as to actually stretch the evidence. They said that my performance appraisals would not support my selection over Jack in the absence of discrimination because my shortcomings had been previously made known to me by management. Therefore, they somehow concluded from this fact not in evidence that Jack and I were not evenly matched with race being the only differential. They even went so far as to attack their own departmental statistics by claiming that the numbers we had presented did not show a poor performance of promoting blacks to higher grade levels. Yet they failed to point to a single instance of a black employee having been promoted to any of the two grade levels above GS-13 or to the elite Senior Executive Service.

My attorney's response to the appeal was a forceful exposition on its basic weakness. No law had been erroneously interpreted and no pertinent case had been offered by the government as a precedent supporting any claim of legal transgression. To simply claim that facts in evidence were unsupportive of a conclusion was not the same thing as proving that there had been violations of legal precepts. She agreed with several of their statements of the law, such as the fact that pre-selection is not, of itself, illegal. Then, she went on to cite several ruling cases which said that pre-selection was, however, entirely relevant to the discriminatory intent of a selecting official. In this manner, she savaged each of the government's claims with documented rejection of the notion that the law had not been properly followed. The entire appeal, her final statement opined, was nothing more than a laborious re-arguing of every issue it had raised earlier and offered not a single attack on anyone's interpretation of the law.

On July 10, 1990, the Office of Review and Appeals firmly and at great length in their opinion rejected Commerce's Request to Reopen. This ruling ended the last opportunity of the government to administratively oppose my claim of racial discrimination in promotion. Accordingly, EEOC issued an order to NOAA to promote me to the position of regional manager at a grade level of GS-14 and to issue the appropriate back pay and benefits due, along with payment of my attorney's fees — a clear and present victory at last!

The part of the order that I enjoyed every bit as much as the promotion was the section that required the agency to conspicuously post a notice in the office that a violation of Title VII of the Civil Rights Act of 1964, as amended, had occurred at the facility. The notice was specifically ordered to recite a statement that federal law requires that there be no discrimination against any employee or applicant for employment because of a person's RACE, COLOR, RELIGION, SEX, NATIONAL ORIGIN, AGE, OR PHYSICAL OR MENTAL HANDICAP with respect to hiring, firing, promotion, compensation or other terms, conditions, or privileges of employment. Even the use of capital letters was required in the order. For 60 days, this message would have to hang in conspicuous places where every employee and visitors to the office could see it. It was the bureaucratic equivalent of Hawthorne's scarlet letter.

The decision, and especially the public notice, were embarrassments to the office management and specifically to the 11 individuals who had testified against me. Tony, of course, had left the office, so I should perhaps refer to them as "the gang of ten." In effect, there was now hanging on their own walls a public declaration that they had violated the law and then lied about it.

With the publication of the order and posting of the required notice there came a new attitude toward Eric Hughes in the office. When I would encounter Edward or any member of the gang of ten, each would do his or her best to deport themselves as if there had been no important event in recent office history. They did their best to act as though unaffected by the decision. Most of them even attempted cordiality toward me. Even white employees who had taken no part in my case evidenced a sense of respect that had not been previously noticeable to me. I did not expect and did not receive any congratulations from them. But they became more willing to speak and even to sit down to discuss work-related issues. In general, they returned my calls faster and began to return my draft evaluations on time. Most important to my work, they began to coordinate in the proper manner and to no longer undercut me in meetings with state officials.

This is not to report that suddenly all was forgiven and forgotten by everybody. More than 30 years of government service in an atmosphere of pervasive racial discrimination had placed forgiveness beyond my capacities and I could never forget the principal perpetrators. Moreover, I knew that no amount of self-imposed temporary cordiality would mask the true feelings of those who hated me for insisting on treatment as if I was one of their equals. I still had to work with these people, however, and carrying a chip on my shoulder would only be counterproductive to whatever real or feigned collegiality might be possible in these new circumstances. So I became rededicated to my work. In fact, I believe some of the best evaluation documents I ever produced were done shortly after the final decision because it was the first time I had worked in that position in an atmosphere unfettered by outrageous duress.

If the order to promote me to regional manager had been specifically carried out, I would have been thrust into a position under Edward's daily direct supervision. Even though both of us were currently doing everything possible to maintain correct professional relations, we were, at best, undergoing an armed truce on a fairly bloody battlefield. I was not afraid of Edward, but I knew from years of observing him in action that he was an inherently vindictive individual who would not suffer humiliation for very long. To place myself in a situation where conflict between us would be almost inevitable was something I neither wanted nor needed.

I, therefore, negotiated an agreement with my supervisor, Alice, to stay on her staff as a GS-14. Since evaluators were top-graded at GS-13, Alice had to work out a new title. Alice got the personnel office to approve two new positions with the new title, senior, evaluation team leader, which carried a GS-14 grade level. My new position was one of these posts.

There was also a slot titled evaluation officer which carried a GS-14 grade level and had been vacant for some time because Alice was acting in that position in addition to her other duties as chief of our division. Theoretically, the vacant position of evaluation officer involved supervision of a staff of four evaluators who reported to Alice. The most obvious solution would have been for Alice to promote me to the vacant GS-14 slot she had been acting in for so long. I wondered why she had created two new positions instead.

Also serving under Alice was a white fellow named Albert, a GS-13, who had a master's degree in planning and had about the same time and experience in the office as I did. There had never been any friction between Albert and me, so I had no sense of apprehension a few months later when Alice invited both of us into her office. She explained that because of her increasing workload, she was going to have to fill the vacant post of evaluation officer. Without making a commitment, she gave every indication that Albert would be promoted to the post. Since the table of organization for our division showed that all evaluators reported to the evaluation officer, it looked as if I was about to get another white man promoted over me.

Sure enough, a week later, Alice promoted Albert to the grade of GS-14 with the title of evaluation officer. Albert, who had neither asked for nor earned the position, was suddenly promoted on a non-competitive basis to be my new boss. By stretching the personnel rules and not posting the position for competitive applications, Alice had prevented me from applying and thereby avoided a discrimination charge which I would have filed if I had applied for the job and been turned down. Of course I could have filed a complaint anyway and, perhaps, might have won on nothing more than claiming that the action had been an example of retaliation against me by management. It was just one more dreary example of the lengths to which white people will go to deny black people an opportunity and respect. In the end, I decided not to take action. The offense had been more typical than serious and my energy level for such pursuits was particularly depleted at that time.

Toward the end of 1990, a new director, Bertha, was appointed to head the Office of Ocean and Coastal Resources Management.

Bertha had come to us from an environmental organization in Rhode Island that had coordinated closely with the office for years. So, she was quite familiar with our mission and management. She was fully aware of the fiefdom manner in which Edward and Tony had managed the office and knew all about my successful discrimination complaint.

As if to prove her knowledge of office problems, the first official act Bertha took was to remove Edward from a position of power. He eventually took a position in another program out of the office. Shortly thereafter, she had Sylvia re-assigned out of the office. With these two actions alone, Bertha gained the loyalty of all the staff, white and black, as well as that of most state officials who dealt with us. For the first time in memory, everyone could do their jobs without looking over their shoulder to see if an action might somehow become cause for another sneaky, vindictive action from Edward or one of his office toadies.

For the next five years, I served as senior evaluation team leader. During this period, I produced effective and comprehensive program evaluations and made many recommendations which were well received by state and office managers. I was able to work cooperatively with our division staff, conducted training courses for new employees and took on a number of new challenges.

A major continuing irritant, however, was that Alice would never give me an outstanding performance appraisal rating. Like every other manager in the office, she had been fully aware that one of the things which lost the case for Tony and Edward was the fact that, after giving me outstanding ratings, they tried to claim I had been under performing. Alice was making sure that the same couldn't happen to her.

After three years of receiving less than outstanding performance ratings, I brought up the matter with a manager senior to Alice. He said that Alice might simply be unaware of the things I did during an appraisal period and suggested that I document each meritorious action during a single period and discuss them with her at appraisal time. Even though I felt that Alice was fully aware of my actions and was operating from a non-work related agenda, I decided to go ahead and take the advice. Each day, I would list significant actions taken. Sometimes there would be ten daily entries on my list and other times only a few. But I wrote down every one. It was actually a good experience for me because I came to realize that I was getting more accomplished than I had formerly recognized. At the end of the next performance appraisal period, I presented Alice with 35 pages of single-spaced, recorded achievements and suggested we discuss each of them. The long talk proved unnecessary and she rated my performance as outstanding.

Asking the unanswerable question is an unproductive enterprise, but sometimes a black man can only look up to the sky and ask, "What do I have to do to get treated the same as everyone else?"

As it turned out, I couldn't even gracefully retire without additional insults. In 1995, the Clinton administration authorized the Office of Personnel Management to offer early retirement buy-out programs to employees with service in excess of 30 years. It was part of the effort to reduce the size of government.

I accepted the buy-out plan and was preparing to leave when Alice asked me to stay an additional month. I hadn't completed the Delaware evaluation and she was quite concerned it wouldn't get done properly if I didn't finish it myself. I put aside the personal plans my wife and I had made and stayed the extra month to complete the evaluation. It would have been routine in such cases for a manager to make some small action, such as a minor award or citation for the record, by way of saying thank you. There is no doubt in my mind that Alice would have done that for a white person who performed a similar service. In my case, of course, she said and did nothing.

Each year, the office hosts a national meeting of program managers in Washington. The purpose of the three-day conference is to get all managers and staff together to discuss, in meetings and workshops, coastal resources and estuarine reserve program issues. There are also dinners and social events. The number of participants ran around 200 whites and eight or nine blacks. About two-thirds of the whites in attendance were state personnel and the rest were federal staff from our office. At the end of my career, I had spent 15 years in the office. I may have known and worked with more state personnel than anyone else because I had worked in two different divisions and two regions.

The last national meeting I attended was in February 1995. I had just informed a new director that I had accepted a buy-out and would be leaving soon. Generally, the tone of these meetings is upbeat. The plenary session is, traditionally, a time when the exceptional deeds of managers and staff are announced for recognition. Many times, I have heard the director announce the retirement of professional employees and say a few kind words on their service. Neither the director nor any other executive mentioned my coming retirement.

After the conference, the word got around to the state coastal managers and their staffs that I was leaving federal service. I was most pleased to then receive phone calls, faxed messages and letters from many of them expressing their appreciation of past cooperation and wishing me happiness in retirement.

A black secretary who serviced our division told me she was directed by Alice to coordinate a farewell office party for me. When she told me, I informed her I did not want one because of the way I was under appreciated as a senior member of Alice's staff. A few days later, I changed my mind and went along with the plan. I was pleasantly surprised by the large turnout. It confirmed that I had many friends in the office even though they did not outwardly show it when Tony and Edward were in charge. Even Betty, one of the 11 agency witnesses at my hearing, attended the party. We had a cordial conversation and wished each other well.

Before leaving, I took the black secretaries and clerks out to lunch (and thereby temporarily deprived the office of nearly every employee of Grade GS-4 and below) for the ostensible purpose of saying goodbye. My underlying purpose was to urge them to get a handle on their careers, go to school, show interest in their work, take on extra assignments and to not ever be bashful in seeking promotions. They knew my history and we had a good talk about blacks working in a white world. The one message I hope I got across to them was my profound belief that the dream can't become reality until we all oppose racial unfairness wherever and whenever it's inflicted upon us.

1990 Reunion with boyhood friends left to right —
Cedric Richardson, Eric Hughes, Larry Bryant and Joseph Davis

Million Man March, October 16, 1995 — Washington, D.C.
left to right — prominent writer and politcal activist,
Imamu Amiri Baraka, Eric Hughes and the late
Gaston Neal, prominent poet and writer

Retirement Party, July 21, 1995

Eric Hughes

Family — left to right — Tracy Holbert, Wendy Hughes, Eric Hughes, Norma Hughes and Chase Watson

Winston Hughes

Calvin Hughes

Cynthia Moore

left to right — Wendy Hughes, Delores Bynoe,
Cynthia Moore and Aaron Hughes

Robert Clark

Walter E. Fauntroy and Eric Hughes

Eric Hughes and Secretary of State Colin Powell
at State's birthday celebration for
Dr. Martin Luther King, Jr., January 23, 2001

The Hughes family

CHAPTER TEN

The story I have told recounts the details of the discrimination that I experienced in the workplace for a number of years. During that process, I learned valuable lessons that were critical to my success in challenging that discrimination. I've distilled the lessons of my story into the following list of practical strategies or more specifically, Things To Do and Things Not To Do. While they are not a panacea for discrimination in general, they could make the difference between winning and losing a case.

THINGS TO DO

A. Before You File A Complaint

1. Be the best employee you can be. This may sound like a cliché, but it's very important! Perform your job at the highest level and maintain a good attitude in the office. Make every attempt to have good relationships with your managers and co-workers.

2. Improve your qualifications at every opportunity by seeking after-hours training, college courses and professional training courses. Make sure that your personnel office receives copies of your educational achievements. Conduct periodic checks of your official personnel file to ensure that all educational achievements are on file and accurate.

3.   Develop an Individual Development Plan indicating what you hope to achieve professionally and when. Then discuss it with your manager.

4.   Be aware of and understand your agency's Equal Employment Office program. All agencies are required to have an affirmative action plan, which is a conscious, deliberate effort to make certain that qualified minority and female employees are given a full and fair opportunity to be represented in – and progress in – the agency's workforce.

     Determine whether affirmative action is being applied to your working unit, in general, and to you in particular. If it is not, write to your manager and agency EEO manager and seek answers about why it is not being implemented in your unit.

5.   Become an active participant in national organizations for the purpose of understanding the depth of what African-Americans are faced with on a daily basis in this country. Be available to help plan the future. The National Association for the Advancement of Colored People, National Urban League, Nation of Islam, Blacks in Government and the Congressional Black Caucus are some of the better-known organizations.

6.   Be aware of and understand that discrimination against blacks in the workplace is still alive and could possibly impact you some day. Understand that it is not something from the past.

Building a Paper Trail

7.   Document daily achievements throughout the year and file them away until your performance appraisal review.

8.   Be a "problem identifier" and "problem solver" in your respective office. Document and share these ideas about problems only in writing with your supervisor.

9. Volunteer for office assignments and participation on committees to help your office reach its goals and objectives and document what you've done.

10. Be aware of the treatment of other employees in the office with respect to opportunities in training, promotions, travel, awards and assignments. Document the disparities when compared to your treatment in the office, particularly the ones you feel are discriminatory.

11. Document conversations, meetings or other encounters pertaining to your status in the office.

12. Maintain copious records of medical visits, sick leave, etc. Aggrieved employees or applicants can collect up to $300,000 in compensatory damages when requesting damages.

Performance Appraisals

13. Ask your manager to provide you with the criteria for receiving an outstanding performance appraisal and pursue it. It could make the difference in your receiving a promotion or other career enhancement opportunities.

14. Present your documented achievements to your manager at the six-month and final performance appraisal reviews. Request a narrative from your manager on "passed" ratings that details at what level your performance passed. This is particularly important when you are being considered for promotions and awards. Ensure that your documentation is reflected in the manager's narrative.

15. Provide your supervisor with documented evidence of your voluntary and participatory achievements and request that they be included in your appraisal. It will show that you are a team player who is interested in helping the office reach its goals and objectives.

16. During the six-month review period, ask your manager for written suggestions for improving your performance

and focus on them during the final six-month period to improve your overall rating.

17.   Challenge performance appraisals you believe are inaccurate or unfair and request, in writing, upgraded appraisals.

Alternative Dispute Resolution

18.   If you have a discrimination complaint and decide to pursue it, you may choose the Alternative Dispute Resolution process (mediation) as a means to resolve your complaint (if your agency offers it). A person can choose ADR in the informal or formal stage in the processing of a case. If ADR is chosen at the formal stage and is not resolved in ADR, a complete investigation is conducted. Note: the processing time can also be extended for 90 days if ADR is chosen.

It is recommended that an attorney be with aggrieved employees or applicants in ADR or at least someone who has knowledge of Title VII and the administrative processing of an EEO complaint.

B.   After You File A Complaint

19.   Filing a discrimination complaint should always be your last resort. If you must file, pursue it until you receive justice. File your complaint within 45 days of the alleged discriminatory act, as stipulated by EEO regulations or it will be thrown out. Do not lose your case on a technicality. Know the EEO deadlines for each segment of your case.

20.   Maintain a psychological advantage as you go through the complaint process and do not fear it. Maintain your dignity and never let them see you sweat. Smile and be courteous at all times.

21.   Remember! The burden of proof is on you, the complainant. Make sure that your complaint is valid and strong. For example, when filing a complaint about

competitive promotions, you must establish by prepon-
derance of the evidence a prima facie case of discrimination, e.g., you are a member of a protected class, you
applied and were qualified for a promotion, you were
considered for, but were denied the promotion, and
other employee(s) with similar qualifications but not
members of your protected class were promoted at the
time your promotion was denied.

22. Cite the discriminatory action that caused you to file
    your complaint and include documentation of other dis-
    criminatory issues you've compiled over time to support
    your chief complaint. The documentation will show the
    discriminatory work environment of your office and
    help your case.

23. Introduce indirect evidence of racial discrimination
    because it is acceptable to demonstrate a manager's pre-
    text (cover-up) actions, e.g., producing relevant statis-
    tics such as the manager's poor record of promoting
    African-Americans to high-level positions and showing
    evidence of a hostile work environment.

24. When the EEO counselor completes a report on your
    formal complaint, review it carefully to ensure the facts
    are accurate. Make certain the counselor corrects all
    inaccuracies before signing off on the report.

25. Review ALL affidavits carefully. For affidavits support-
    ing your case, make certain they are strong and support
    your allegation of discrimination. Ask the investigator to
    re-interview witnesses if you are not comfortable with
    their responses. As for affidavits from witnesses sup-
    porting management's case, review them carefully. If
    the questions and responses are inadequate, develop
    specific questions for them and ask the investigator to
    re-interview the witnesses using YOUR questions.

26. If your case is scheduled to be heard before EEOC, be
    alert and ready to assist your attorney during the entire
    process.

27. Understand clearly that there is no formula or recipe for winning discrimination cases. Each case must be judged on its own merits. It is a very difficult and draining process with no guarantees of success.

Co-worker Issues

28. You must try to get credible co-workers and other employees who have first-hand knowledge of the issues leading up to your complaint, to testify on your behalf. Their testimony will be powerful and one of the most effective means of support.

29. Expect that other employees may be asked by management to spy on you and any negative information gained by them may be used against you.

30. Expect to be ostracized and alienated by co-workers, both black and white. Continue to perform your responsibilities to the best of your ability.

31. Expect that other employees may choose or be told by management to be difficult with you. Continue to maintain as cordial a relationship as possible and do not reciprocate.

32. Support co-workers who are going through the complaint process because you never know when discrimination may impact on your career and you too may need support.

Attorneys

33. When shopping for an attorney, seek one with knowledge and experience under Title VII of the Civil Rights Act of 1964, as amended.

34. Seek a pro bono attorney or volunteer lawyer program willing to provide free legal services to aggrieved employees or applicants who cannot afford an attorney. These programs are available in all 50 states and in most coun-

ties. However, be aware that there are income eligibility guidelines. Check your local program for information.

In addition, check with local law schools for legal assistance. There may be senior law students who would be willing to take on a case for a project. Some professors would also be willing to take on cases as projects.

35.   Some attorneys are willing to take cases on a contingency basis. If you win your case, the attorney receives part of the financial settlement. If you lose your case, the attorney receives nothing.

36.   Be confident that the attorney you choose has your best interests at heart. If you are uncomfortable with the attorney you've selected, consider seeking another before the existing attorney gets too deep into your case.

Choices

37.   Consider going to court with your complaint. Civil actions must be filed within ninety (90) calendar days of the date a complainant receives final action or final decision from the agency, within 90 days after receipt of the EEOC's final decision on appeal, or after 180 days from the date of filing an appeal with the EEOC if there has been no final decision by the Commission (See EEO regulations for stipulations).

38.   Consider filing a class action complaint against your agency if you know of other employees, former employees or applicants who have been adversely affected by your agency's personnel policy or practice which discriminates against the group based on your race, color, religion, sex, national origin, age or disability.

39.   Consider seeking assistance from your local and congressional representatives if your case gets bogged down with delays in processing at the administrative level (either within the allegedly discriminating agency or between the allegedly discriminating agency and EEOC).

THINGS NOT TO DO

1. Don't file baseless discrimination complaints. Make sure the issues are consistent with the provisions under Title VII of the Civil Rights Act of 1964, as amended.

2. Don't hire an attorney until your complaint has been investigated and the agency has made a final decision to dismiss your case. It could save you money. However, if you choose ADR, having an attorney as your representative would be in your best interest.

3. Don't ever assume "this [discrimination] can't happen to me," or "if I mind my business and help no one during their case, I'll be safe and this won't happen to me."

4. Don't refuse to pursue an EEO complaint out of fear of retaliation or because someone threatens you. Report immediately all retaliatory actions by management to your attorney.

5. Don't discuss your case with anyone other than your legal representative or spouse.

6. Don't wait until you have to file a complaint to begin the documentation. It's critical to have documentation to support your case.

7. Don't let the lack of financial resources discourage you from filing a complaint.

8. Don't give up your pursuit for justice. Think of those who gave their lives fighting for civil and human rights in this country.

EPILOGUE

Having had a few years to look back and reflect on my career in the federal government, I've squarely faced the age-old question of whether or not I'd do the major things differently if given the impossible opportunity to face the same challenges again. Being able to say, "No! I would not do otherwise," provides a level of intellectual comfort.

Such thoughts inevitably give rise to the question of why I feel compelled to write my story. Black people, especially younger ones, supposedly need to read the story of role models—the great athletes, movie stars, famous military leaders, renowned clergymen and the host of distinguished members of our race who have conquered all the barriers and reached achievement levels upon which we may found our dreams. With this notion, I have no disagreement. Our lot would be harder indeed if we had no stars in our skies.

At the same time, we must face the fact that out of our many millions, only a very few attain stellar status. What about the common man? No one will ever write about my mother and father. Yet I know for certain that without the role model of their having handled adversity, poverty and discrimination with quiet dignity and unfailing courage, I could never have mustered the strength to oppose a life of mindless insults and the denial of my humanity.

What, you may reasonably ask, is so unusual about that? Almost every black person in America lives his or her life constantly dealing with white rejection. Much has been written of our second burden. The notion goes that all people of every race face the common burden of providing for family, serving the community and so on. That is the first, perhaps, human burden. But the black race suffers the second burden of pervasive racial discrimination in just about every aspect of existence in this country. Why would one ordinary life, spent in a social environment all of us suffer under, be worth writing about? Who wants to read about stuff we all know about already?

The answer is that I believe there is a third burden which few people talk about. Sure, we all know about the reality of the second burden and we don't need anyone to tell about it. If you accept the reality of the second burden, living in a sea of relentless racial bias, then I contend you must take up the third burden of opposing it. To do less keeps all our future generations under a godless yoke that neither they, nor we, deserve. If we refuse to take up this third burden, if we ignore it, deny it, hide from it, leave it to others, or (worst of all) just plain cope with it, we will never be free.

What I call our third burden is not a clarion for leadership or violence. What greater leader will our race ever produce than Reverend King? What good did any of our fiery urban riots produce? How many more laws protecting our civil rights must be written? My answer to these questions is simply, none. All those things are done and don't need to be done again. What's needed now is for the common man and woman, millions of us everywhere, to take up the third burden and live our lives in a manner of constant refusal to accept injustice. We need massive unity of life purpose much more than new leadership or laws.

We, the common soldiers in the trenches, and not our generals, are the only ones who can make the dream a reality for our daughters and sons. It's the toughest possible road to take. My story is only one, but it can be a start. It at least shows that victories are possible for ordinary blacks even if their costs often seem inordinate. Perhaps by just telling about the cost of refusing to accept unfairness, we can help others decide to carry the third burden.

There is continuous stress in relentless opposition. Sometimes it can be unendurable, sometimes it's not hard to handle, but it's always there. Just the fact of having to work every day with people who hate you not only because you're black, but because you're suing them as well, can be very hard to get through. It affects your family, your children and your friends. If your opposition is work-related, it affects your career directly. But since we're fated to carry the second burden, with all its stresses, are we really making things

132

harder by picking up the third? At least by fighting, no matter how hard and long, we're enduring stress that may produce good results. Nothing good can ever come from simply learning to cope with the stress of the second burden alone.

My story may be a coda for a life less than a symphony; but it's been worth telling if it helps spread the idea of massive daily resistance by all of us.

Eric Hughes
Washington, D.C.
August 2002

ADDENDUM
The District of Columbia, Last Colony in America

I have been a citizen of the city which is our national capital for 40 years. When writing this story of my personal battles against unfairness, I could not avoid thinking about the clear parallels between my individual experience and that of all the citizens in my adopted hometown, Washington, D.C. Living here is, in many important ways, an experience in political discrimination, which no objective observer could possibly characterize without commenting on its condition being driven by unspoken white racism. I could not complete my story until I had also written about the life of the city itself.

Shortly after the 13 British colonies won the revolution and formed our nation, the new government created its own colony and named it the District of Columbia. Laid out in the shape of a perfect diamond with four straight ten-mile borders joining at axes pointing North/South and East/West, it was to be the capitol of the United States. Land west of the Potomac River was donated by Virginia and the eastern part ceded by Maryland. Unlike the 13 original states and all those to follow, the District of Columbia was never allowed to declare its sovereignty nor have its citizens ever been granted the voting political franchise regarded as a basic right by all other citizens of the United States. From its conception, the city has been the orphaned political child of Congress and its citizens required to endure full federal taxation without any voting representation in the government. It would be difficult to conceive a more precise definition of colonialism.

For nearly 200 years, the municipal functions of the city were overseen by a commissioner, appointed by the president with the advice and consent of Congress, which was charged with administering local government under the direction of the president and control of the Congress. The citizenry of the city had no voice at all. In the 1960s, when President Lyndon Johnson was getting his civil rights legislation through Congress, he recognized that he could never get the legislature to grant political franchise to a city made up of predominately black Americans. He took the only step he could and unilaterally decreed that the title of city commissioner would thereafter be changed to mayor. In this manner, a black lawyer named Walter Washington became the first person to be called mayor of Washington.

As a practical matter, it was an empty title. Mayor Washington could only preside over a budget produced solely by Congress and had to act without the implicit power of having been selected by the citizens he was serving. On the other hand, the name change had the effect President Johnson intended. It helped fuel a long smoldering fire in the city's populace for self-government. It framed the question, "If we've got a mayor, why can't we elect that person ourselves?"

After several years of public agitation and congressional debate, a home rule charter was enacted by Congress which abolished the commissioner system and permitted the election of a mayor and city council. The charter was a severely flawed franchise and, at best, can be seen as only a genuflection in the direction of principle.

Congress retained final control over the city's budget and the president was given the right to veto any legislation passed by the city council. It granted the right to levy taxes but strictly limited the available tax base.

The devilish details appear to have been written in an effort to ordinate failure. Unlike other cities in America, the right to tax users of city services (two-thirds of those who work in the city do not reside there) was explicitly withheld. The owner of more than half of the land in the city, the federal government, was excluded from taxation and left to make an annual payment in lieu of taxes in whatever amount it might choose. The city was given no control over its judiciary. Every city in America except the District of Columbia enjoys support from the state in which it resides. States nurture their cities by usually providing or substantially subsidizing prisons, mental health facilities, hospitals, pension funds and major road projects. All these matters were left to the city, alone, without any recourse mechanisms except the whims of Congress.

Granted such a structure of government, the city was forced to steadily raise local taxes to pay for services. This had a predictable effect of driving out many of the middle class citizens. Since the passage of so-called home rule, the population of the District of Columbia has declined to below 600,000 from an initial home rule base of more than 800,000. As people left the city, the cost of services had to be shared by increasingly fewer citizens. Streets were not being swept, trash was not being picked up regularly and one of the significant results was a dirty nation's capitol and a damaged public image.

By the mid-1990s, the city could no longer pay its bills. Congress appointed a control board to oversee all financial matters. This event was used by racists as a proclamation that African-Americans were not capable of self-government. Having legislated an impossible structure of government, the white Congress then proceeded to blame its failure on its unenfranshised black citizenry.

A whole range of cures have been proposed – everything from giving the non-federal portion of the city back to Maryland (the land initially given to the District by Virginia was returned many years ago), to granting the city statehood. Each suggestion meets a political brick wall. The Republicans claim that they don't want to create a state made up almost entirely of Democrats and Maryland claims it can't support another city. In all such claims, however, the underlying issues of racism are very thinly veiled. Can anyone seriously doubt that if the city were made up of whites it would not quickly be given real self-government and federal voting representation?

In a very real way, my long struggle against racial discrimination replicates the history of the very city in which I have lived most of my adult life. The conclusion is also the same. Real change cannot come about until each American respects and honors the full constitutional rights of every other citizen without regard to race.